Diverse Threads: Everyday Anecdotes

By

Rtn Sudhir Sharma

January 2024

Prologue

In the quiet corners of our lives, amidst the daily routines and ordinary moments, extraordinary stories unfold. Diverse Threads: Everyday Anecdotes is a collection of true events and incidents that remind me of different times and places where I stayed during the last four decades. I behold several anecdotes of different genres, experienced during a long and fulfilling career. Some of these are related to work and others not. I chose to include in this assortment the ones which are of a common sort and could have happened to anyone at some point in time. Some of these are inspiring, some interesting, some not-so-interesting, others informational, some may be funny and others somewhat spooky even!

During my work-related movement to various places in India and abroad, my wife and I had a chance to meet and interact with individuals from different backgrounds providing a firsthand experience of diversity in local traditions, festivals, work culture, thought processes and much more. It is always a great pleasure to work in diverse environments. Getting acquainted with different cultures, perspectives, and lifestyles facilitates developing new skills, builds knowledge and broadens your outlook that comes handy in your path ahead. Knowing about the culture and customs of the people you are working with enables you to build stronger relationships and work more effectively as a team. The anecdotes are from this long journey though not necessarily related to or influenced by the local factors. Given my professional background in the public sector corporate realm, I am mindful that the Section-II anecdotes in this collection may resonate more with fellow public sector executives while the Section-I anecdotes are of a general genre. I have tried to keep the depiction concise and crisp tracking the natural flow of events as they had happened in each of the incidents. Effort is made to make these interesting reads during your leisure time, if you are still in the habit of reading in these times of several other e-distractions. You will enjoy reading these anecdotes more if you try to put yourself in my boots while reading them. Prepare to be captivated by the intriguing, heartwarming and unforgettable tales of real-life moments and celebrate the beauty of the human experience.

Enjoy!

Rtn Sudhir Sharma

Content

Prologue

Section-I Everyday Chronicles

Section-II Corporate Dynamics

Epilogue

Section-I Everyday Chronicles

Haunted Street

January 1985- I was running against time to complete a time bound project report. Throughout my career, I prided myself on adhering to deadlines, thanks to some divine interventions that spared me the need to request extensions. On this day, it was past four o'clock in the evening when I finished writing the last chapter of the report and I felt like having a steaming cup of coffee to rejuvenate myself. More so, because I had skipped lunch in order not to break the continuity of the thought process while penning down the concluding part of the report. Traversing the long corridors of the Institute, I entered the cafeteria which wore a desolate look. At this hour in the month of January, it starts getting a little dark, cold and gloomy. Moreover, as it was past tea-time of 3 pm, there wasn't anybody in the cafeteria.

 I walked over to the cash counter, made payment, and collected my favourite black coffee and a couple of chocolate cookies. As I turned back to look for a place to sit and relax, I noticed Ravi- a good friend sitting in the extreme corner with a rather lost look on his face- normally a cheerful youngster always full of energy. I thought of sitting with him for a while. He greeted me as he looked at me approaching him. I asked him what was bothering him but he smiled dryly and said there wasn't anything amiss. We chatted for a while but he looked a little disturbed to me – not at all his normal self. Finishing my coffee, I prepared to leave, but Ravi, with a hesitant demeanor, called me back. In a low voice he asked me if he could borrow my camera for about a week. He knew that I had a Yashica Electro-35 camera since I had bought this in Dhanbad last year when we were together doing M.Tech in Petroleum Exploration – I as an ONGC sponsored candidate and Ravi as a fresher. After completion of his studies, he had got a job in ONGC and was posted in the Institute at Dehradun. He was then a bachelor and stayed in a new society off Chakrata Road.

Little did I know that this seemingly innocuous request would lead us down a path intertwined with the shadows of a haunted street. Since Ravi had never asked for the camera before, a little curious I asked him what he required it for, even half-jokingly I said who's the lucky girl for the date- must be pretty photogenic, isn't it. He wasn't amused at all and looked hesitant to divulge anything. But he said that he would tell me everything later. Not thinking much, I told him to collect it from my house that day itself while leaving the office. That evening he picked up the camera and the flash from my apartment. We didn't meet for the next 3-4 days after that. Later, one fine day – probably the following Saturday we bumped into each other again. This instance, he was composed, vibrant and his usual self. We sat over a cup of coffee again at his favourite corner table. That day he told me the reason why he borrowed the camera.

Alkapuri where he lived as a tenant was a society under development with very few houses inhabited, some under construction, plenty of open spaces with mango and lichee orchards and some big trees as well. Although the street running through the society had streetlights, they seldom worked. As the sun dipped below the horizon, the soceity assumed an eerie silence, especially during the winter months when the chill hung in the air. During those times, a trend was emerging among homeowners in burgeoning societies like this one- they opted to construct compact one or two-room units at the rear or on the first floor, designed specifically for renting to bachelors or small families. This not only secured the house during the owner's absence but also brought in additional income in the form of monthly rent. Dehradun, with its scenic beauty, carried a notorious reputation for petty thefts and daytime burglaries, making such precautions a prudent choice.

Ravi told me a spine-chilling incident that happened last week when a friend of his who lived nearby in another one-room unit was to visit Delhi on a vacation. He had booked a seat on the night bus which left Dehradun at 11.30 pm. The bus stand was just 15 minutes' drive from their society so Ravi had offered to drop him at the bus stand last Friday night on his bike- a brand new Yezdi. They had decided to leave at 11 pm to reach the bus stand well in time. It was a cold and frosty, dark January night with a light drizzle that added an element of mystique to the atmosphere while the area lay shrouded under a blanket of fog. Foggy nights during the cold season are very usual for Dehradun but this, topped with no streetlights makes the scene quite scary straight out of a Stephen King horror story. In such conditions, even when streetlights are working, little difference is made as the dense fog obliterates the glow of the lamps.

As Ravi was outside his house sharp at 11 pm waiting for his friend, he noticed that the eerie silence of the chilly night was broken only by the distant barks of a dog or by occasional hooting of an owl perched somewhere on a nearby tree declaring nonchalantly his claim of the territory to the other intruding owls. As Ravi was looking at his wristwatch, his friend came out of his house with a backpack, locked it and was ready to leave for the bus stand. But before leaving, he rang the doorbell of his house owner who lived in the front portion and told him of his outbound programme.

The duo kicked off their journey on Ravi's roaring bike, venturing into the foggy night. After covering a mere hundred meters, a spectral figure appeared on the road ahead—a ghostly vision of a lady in a flowing white gown, seemingly gliding towards them. Ravi slammed the brakes, the bike screeching to a halt as the engine fell silent. The ghostly sight paralyzed them with fear, a real-life encounter with the supernatural amid the darkness they had only read about in horror tales. Aghast by the very sight, he didn't know what to do. Their hearts were galloping at this sudden unexpected sight of what looked like a ghost. Both the friends were panicky, getting jitters and chills. Suddenly, the thought of missing the bus crossed their minds and not really knowing what to do, Ravi started the bike, switched on the headlights, and revved the engine to shoo away the ghostly figure but the figure was unnerved and kept gliding towards them. As if all this wasn't enough, a flock of bats probably attracted by the bike's headlights started flying around them squeaking and squawking through the floating fog. Ravi's friend was almost freaking out. It was frightening, their hearts pounding and faces ashen grey, they were in a fix- they couldn't have turned back or else they would miss the bus but they were too scared to move ahead.

They nervously glanced at each other as the distance between the floating white figure and themselves was getting shorter with every passing moment. Being youngsters, the two of them together, finally mustered the courage to move on and confront the spooky figure if need be. As they started to move, there was an abrupt gust of wind and they noticed that figure moving towards them on the left side of the road had now shifted to the right side of the road. With their hearts stuck in their throats, they drove past her, trying not to meet her gaze. They caught a side glance of her and it looked like a rather long face with an unsettling grin which kept turning as if staring at them constantly as they sped past.

They couldn't see her face clearly because it was drizzling and the face had a bright halo by the side which had blurred their vision. Reaching a little ahead they stopped to look back but by then the figure had melted into the darkness. They waited there under a tree for a while to catch their breath. To their utter surprise, they saw her emerging out of nowhere at a distance where she had vanished. It had now started raining and the spooky white figure was now moving at a fast pace- almost running back towards them. Shaken to the core, without hanging out there even for a moment, they drove away and in another hundred meters they hit the main road which was properly lit and they finally reached the bus station. Their hearts still pounding rapidly and throats parched, they parked the bike in one corner of the premises and dashed to the nearest tea stall.

They had come out unscathed from this frightening and eerie encounter. Ravi's friend boarded the bus but the big dilemma before Ravi was how to get back to his house alone in the dead of night after having an experience that was paranormal, Ravi was thinking. He finally stayed the night with a friend who lived in the city.

Ravi was shaken by this incident but wanted to get to the bottom of it. The big question was whether it was really a ghost or just an illusion or something else. His logic was that if it was a paranormal activity then the spooky white figure would not be captured in a camera and the camera roll would remain blank. He had read somewhere that anything that was captured by a camera cannot be paranormal. He told me that another friend of his, who also lived nearby, had experienced a similar sighting once before but the spooky figure had turned back and vanished as he approached her on his bike. So, they both decided to enact a Sherlock Holmes to get to the bottom of this mystery. That day also it was a similar situation- dense fog, cold night and light drizzle. Ravi with a friend sat hidden in the bushes once and behind a boundary wall the other time. They failed to notice any paranormal activity on the first day but on the second instant they spotted it at a distance. As she was slowly gliding past them, though they were nervous, they hurriedly clicked a few photographs from a close distance in that haze since Ravi was determined to resolve the matter. Since it was not a digital camera, they couldn't see the results instantly.

Next day Ravi received a call on his office phone from his friend who had gone to Delhi. He told him that he had extended his stay and would come back after another 2-3 days. He requested Ravi to convey this message to his house owner also, which Ravi did the very next morning. While he was talking to the house owner, their house maid arrived. On seeing Ravi sitting there she asked him, "Sir, your friend hasn't come back yet, when is he due to arrive. I had seen you when you were going to drop him last Friday night."

Surprised, Ravi inquired where had she seen them in the late hours of last Friday night. She told Ravi that she lived in a small settlement called 'Khala' adjacent to where this street meets the main road and sometimes when she's unable to sleep she comes out for a short walk. She further said, "On that day I saw both of you on your bike in the dense fog and light drizzle. Initially, I didn't know that it was you on the bike. Since it was pitch dark and very foggy, seeing a bike approaching at that hour, I got scared and I immediately crossed the road to the other side and I flashed a torch light to see who was on the bike, Sir. When I saw you both, I understood that you are going to drop your friend at the bus stand. I went a little ahead and then the drizzle became worse, so I immediately turned back and ran towards my house and saw you both also speeding away from under the tree."

Ravi said that he couldn't help but burst out laughing. The mystery of the haunted street was solved by the 'ghost' herself!

But the story didn't end here. Ravi had returned the camera to me but it still had nearly 18 unexposed frames. On a subsequent visit to Mussoorie, I captured a few good frames after it had snowed there. The film roll, entrusted to the local photographer for developing and printing, probably held the key to an unforeseen mystery. Four days later when the prints materialized, an unsettling revelation emerged – four of them remained ominously blank! Ravi, upon confirmation acknowledged having captured only four photographs that mysterious night.

The enigmatic question lingered: Who this maid was? Quite disconcerting, eh?

Spousal Stall- My Biased Car

In the sweltering August of 1990, Silchar welcomed us with open arms—or at least that's what we thought. A town on the banks of River Barak, nestled in the northeastern heart of India, Silchar promised a four-year adventure for my family- my wife, our three-year-old and a mere two-month-old toddler. On reaching the town and staying there for a couple of days in the Hotel we initially got a cultural shock. Finding a house to our liking here during those days was a challenge as most of the houses were very basic, had small rooms mostly in a hostel like fashion and washrooms either common or outside the buildings. Water connection and sewerage facilities were less common. Landlords proudly flaunted their 'pokhri,' a small pond supplying water for everything from bathing to cooking. Though newer constructions were there but less in number and always in great demand. Silchar is the headquarters of the Cachar district of the state of Assam.

Despite the town's historical roots dating back to Captain Thomas Fisher's 1832 shift of Cachar district headquarters to Janiganj in Silchar, modern amenities were elusive. Silchar, a sleepy town, is surrounded by numerous tea gardens and the famous Cachar Club established by the Britishers which used to be the meeting point for tea-planters. Silchar earned the nickname "Island of Peace" during seventies from Mrs. Indira Gandhi, the then Prime Minister of India, being the only peaceful spot surrounded by areas infested with extremists from various radical groups. Silchar is also the site of the world's first polo club and the first competitive polo match was played here. In 1985, an Air India flight from Kolkata to Silchar became the world's first all-women crew flight!

We finally settled in a house on the slight outskirts of Silchar, primarily since it was a house that had municipal water supply and a colleague of mine Anirudh was already staying in this very campus with his wife and a small son. A couple of tea garden managers and local families became our newfound friends, helping us navigate Silchar's unique charm. Weekends unfolded as mini adventures, exploring the lush greenery and gentle hills that embraced the town. My brand-new Maruti 800, the pride of our journeys, played a central role. Silchar had just one agency for Maruti Cars and I visited them for the periodic service needs.

Being a new buy, I had not had any mechanical issues with the Car in the first two years but then it started giving trouble that too of a weird kind- it would run normally if I were alone in the Car, I noticed. Surprisingly, when my wife would sit beside me, the ride would become jerky and more often, it would stop after travelling a little distance. It was very annoying, especially to my wife- twice it so happened that we had to abandon the trip because of this problem or had to use my scooter. Though the scooter rides were enjoyable but with two children on board on the narrow streets of the city and that too, when dressed up for a get-together, looked more like an adventure.

I took the Car to the service centre and they, after a thorough examination, declared the car in perfect health. That evening, skeptical but determined, we embarked on a trip to a nearby tea garden to visit friends there. The tea garden was about 16 kms away, almost midway on the road to the Airport across a forest and used to be deserted during the late hours. I sat in the car with the boys on the rear seat and the moment my wife sat beside me, the Car engine hesitated momentarily but picked up in a little while. We had barely moved out of the city and the engine started misfiring and the driving became jerky. I somehow continued to drive with my foot firmly on the accelerator even though with some jolts, jerks and bumps- imagine in a new car!

We were about 5 kilometers short of our destination on the state highway when it started pouring like cats and dogs. As if this was not enough, the car also came to a halt suddenly with a jolt. It was pitch dark in the middle of the forest road. I took an umbrella, got out of the car and opened the bonnet. Since I knew quite a bit about car engines, of course as a hobby, I tried to fiddle with the carburettor and electrical system with a torch light in one hand, a screwdriver in the other and the umbrella held pressed under my neck.

The rain became heavier and a gust of wind blew away the umbrella leaving me totally drenched. But I managed to start the engine and drove off- we all had a sigh of relief once we reached the tea estate, safe and sound. We enjoyed the evening with our friends, decided to stay overnight in their guest house and ventured back the next forenoon, with renewed spirits.

On the second visit to the service Station, the Maruti engineer present there felt sorry as he couldn't find the fault since earlier that day the car was running very well. Since Maruti was relatively new with a more sophisticated, new generation, high speed engine compared to more common Fiat and Ambassador cars, he decided to refer the case to Maruti's technical team. He discussed the entire issue with the Maruti team in Gurgaon over a trunk call and they confirmed before me that the SOP being followed in Silchar was ok but decided to keep the car in the workshop for another day. In the evening the car was back running, as smoothly as ever but the moot issue remained unresolved- the moment my wife would sit, the car would throw in a tantrum!

My biased Car

A friend visited us in the evening, one of those days. Determined to unravel the mystery, I asked him to sit beside me to check whether it was my wife only that the car was not accepting or was it anybody sitting on the left front seat that made it behave abnormally. The moment this guy sat next to me on the front passenger seat, the car kicked off its familiar theatrical performance! Relief washed over me like a wave. With newfound evidence, I hurried back to share the revelation with my wife, who wasted no time in firing back, "See, it wasn't me after all!" The car, it seemed, had a penchant for a peculiar performance.

Now a colossal challenge loomed before me- where to get it diagnosed and repaired. Imagine just a two-year-old car which had done less than 5000 kms throwing up such tantrums that were grossly out of proportion. Out of my interest in the car and two-wheeler engines, I had been in the habit of reading related books since my younger days. I remember there were a few Russian books in English on automobile engineering in British Council Library in Lucknow which I had read from time to time. I was a regular visitor to this Library. Interestingly, on my journey to Silchar, I had picked up the car's repair manual from the dealer's showroom in Delhi. This proved to be a stroke of luck, as the manual offered a comprehensive, step-by-step guide to disassembling and reassembling critical electrical and fuel line components.

I decided to dedicate the weekend to resolving the mystery. Armed with my trusty toolkit and the repair manual, I removed the carburettor from the Car. I took a big sheet of paper, placed the carburettor over it and started dismantling it part by part in a very methodical way, colour coding them with the marker pens. I was conversant with the simpler Carburettor of my good old Fiat but this was a different beast altogether. After about two hours of meticulous work, I reassembled it and reinstalled it in the car, only to find that the problem persisted.

Undeterred, I shifted my focus to the car's electrical system. As I disconnected and removed components and wires, a eureka moment struck. The wire connecting to the current distributor had a broken connector, loosely held in its protective rubber housing. The culprit unmasked! Employing a 'jugaad' (a makeshift fix), I removed the connector and directly secured the wire into the distributor and just like that, the problem vanished.

It turned out that when someone sat on the passenger seat, the car tilted slightly to the left because of the weight of the passenger, disrupting the loose wire due to the broken connector. When unoccupied, the wire remained loosely connected. A trivial issue had plunged us into an automotive misery. The Maruti technicians were stumped, but my jugaad had saved the day! It made me reflect on the simplicity of my old Fiat, with its straightforward design and direct connections.

In the end, *all's well that ends well*! We still share a hearty laugh at the memory of our car that refused to start whenever the lady of the house took the passenger seat!

An Uncanny Resemblance

In the early nineties, during my stint in Silchar, the annual pilgrimage to our hometown and other places became a much-anticipated event, courtesy of the Leave Fare Assistance (LFA)- a paid holiday, you can say. This was vital especially for those who were posted in far flung areas and required a break from the routine. During one such trip in 1992, we were to board the Silchar-Calcutta (now Kolkata) flight on the way to Lucknow. Only one daily flight of Indian Airlines was operational on Kolkata-Imphal-Silchar-Kolkata route. Since it was a hopping flight there were no seat numbers allotted.

A mere one hour and fifteen minutes in the air, but the journey occasionally flirted with turbulence, thanks to air pockets over the Bangladesh skies. Whenever we travelled, we preferred to sit together as our little ones got uneasy during turbulence and descent of the aircraft. In those days, for security reasons, the baggage was identified by passengers on the tarmac at the time of boarding before being loaded in the aircraft.

Our strategy was simple- as soon as the boarding announcement echoed through the airport, my wife, with our younger son, would leap onto the aircraft to secure three adjacent seats. Meanwhile, I played the baggage investigator at the tarmac ensuring our belongings were identified and then I would board the flight with the elder son.

This time also, we did the same drill, but being festival season, the flight was full. While looking for my wife in the aircraft after boarding the flight, I was very warmly greeted by a young flight purser. With a broad smile on his face, and seeing the 4-year-old with me, he asked me if I was travelling with my family and how many seats had I booked. He immediately got three seats cleared in the very first row requesting the two passengers to move to other seats.

He then called up the air hostess at the rear end on intercom to send 'one *Mrs. Sharma who is wearing a maroon printed dress with a toddler in her lap'* to the front row. I had given him the description of her attire. The efficiency was nothing short of impressive, a stark contrast to the carrier's reputation that had often taken a few jabs. I thanked the gentleman profusely. Just a few days before, I had chanced upon a newspaper piece featuring the Indian Airlines CEO's commitment to enhancing their inflight services. Little did I expect to witness the wheels of change turning so swiftly. I was appreciative of the pace at which things were organized and implemented.

As the engines roared to life and the flight ascended, the cabin transformed into a haven of *'service with a smile.'* The refreshments were served with astounding hospitality. About half an hour before the landing time, the flight purser approached me and asked, "Sir, is there any update on my request" leaving me puzzled. I didn't understand and asked him to elaborate. That's when he dropped the bombshell – a month ago, on the same route, I supposedly promised him a job at some company where he had applied. Baffled, I explained to him that my last travel out of Silchar by flight was more than six months back and that I had never seen or met him before. Undeterred, he insisted that I was the one who made the commitment. It dawned on me – a case of mistaken identity and told him so very plainly. To convince him, I also told him my name and my workplace. He was indeed dejected but neither I nor he could help it! We parted on a good note after landing at Kolkata Airport but the smile on his face this time lacked the brilliance, poor fellow I felt a twinge of pity for him.

We had a nice vacation at Lucknow and Dehradun and returned to Silchar, fifteen days later. Unlike most other work centres of ONGC, Silchar didn't have the Company's exclusive residential complex, so the officers posted here live scattered in the city on rented accommodations. We were lucky to have a few good friends with in ONGC and a couple of them from the tea gardens. We generally would socialize during the weekends with one or sometimes more families to have the joy of shared moments.

One such family stayed close by – husband, wife and a small kid. We would often meet on weekends either at ours or at their place and have dinner together. The two families were quite compatible and enjoyed meeting each other. That day, the lady seemed peeved with me for being shockingly rude to her. First, I thought that she was kidding but she complained that she waved at me from her first-floor balcony when she saw me travelling in a cycle rickshaw on the road next to their house and to her dismay, I hadn't reciprocated the gesture. I told her that it wasn't me and that she was sadly mistaken but she refused to believe me. Actually, that day, I was at the drill-site some 30 kms away from the town. On knowing this, she said OK but looked reluctant to accept my alibi! Undeterred, I tried to reason with her- why would I ignore her friendly wave and why would I travel in a cycle rickshaw especially when I had a scooter, a personal car, and an official vehicle at my disposal? Incidentally, cycle rikshaws were the only mode of public transport in those days in Silchar barring a few buses.

Slowly, understanding dawned on her and she seemed to relent. She now looked convinced but muttered, "If it wasn't you then who this guy was who had an uncanny resemblance with you." She was now aghast, with her eyes widened realizing the fact that she had beckoned at a stranger and was flustered about the fact that what this guy would be thinking of her!

This tale of the uncanny resemblance doesn't end here- the saga continued. Another such interesting incident happened during the following rainy season. It was raining heavily that morning, so I walked down to my office with an umbrella since my residence was close by. At around 10.30 am I was summoned by the Chief Mr. Kothe, a fine gentleman and a great boss. The moment I entered his office he almost yelled at me- how dare I leave him in the middle of the road and speed away even when he had signalled me to wait for him. In Silchar, except for the main roads, the by-lanes weren't mettled and during rains these by-lanes made up of red clay used to become so sticky that if you are not careful while walking, your shoe would get stuck and you may fall.

Mr. Kothe lived about 3 kms away from our office and the 100 m approach road to his house was made up of red clay. He had an official white SUV-Gypsy at his disposal. That day the Gypsy didn't report till 9.30 am so he decided to walk down the approach road. That's when he saw a white Gypsy pulling up on the main road and he saw '*me*' sitting in it. So, he signalled '*me*' to wait for him there. While moving carefully on the wet clayey road, constantly looking down maneuvering the bad road, he reached the main road but by then the Gypsy had vanished, it wasn't there. In those days mobile phones were unheard of. He waited for '*me*' there for some time then took a cycle rickshaw to reach the Main Office which was on the way, got another vehicle from there and arrived in the office.

His ire was genuine- the Chief, aged 55 years tells his subordinate to wait for him and his subordinate vanishes in his official car, leaving him high and dry on a rainy day! It's annoying, indeed. Since this was the third incident of this kind of mistaken identity involving me, I knew immediately that it was the same guy- my clone, who had struck once again. I tried to explain to Mr. Kothe the look-alike theory. This added fuel to the fire as he thought that I was pulling a fast one on him, it was like adding insult to injury! His temper flayed and I was in a grim situation. At the same time, I was really feeling bad for him since he was a very kind-hearted person.

 I wanted to calm him down and gave him multiple logical reasons like, when I live within walking distance from the office, what would I be doing in his official Gypsy early in the morning around his house. Moreover, had that been me, why would I leave him in a situation like that, I would rather have grabbed that opportunity to have the privilege of travelling with him to the office. And so on. As I noticed that he had started seeing some sense in my explanations, his official driver barged in, apologizing that the Gypsy broke down in the morning and he tried to inform him by phone from the Transport Control Room but his landline phone was dead. So, he got it repaired, went to his residence and not finding him there he had now reported to the office. Mr. Kothe, now knowing the truth, was nodding his head with a wry smile on his face and his signature frown pretending to be still annoyed. He offered me a seat and ordered hot tea for both of us. I then narrated to him the earlier two incidents and we had a hearty laugh! He told me to read *'The Second Lady'* by *Irving Wallace* which I did – a story of a Russian look-alike of the first lady of the US!

They say that every human being on this Earth has seven look-alikes. Though I never met the one in Silchar but there are six more to be discovered on this Earth! *Even now, sometimes my wife asks me whether I am 'I' or that look-alike of mine!*

The Slippery Burglar

Let me regale you with another tale from the sleepy town of Silchar. Being in the northeastern nooks of the country and since we have only one time zone across the entire country, the sunrise and sunset times adhered to the Indian Standard Time. So, we'd be plunged into darkness by 5.30 pm during the evenings. In the early nineteen nineties when we were there, what made the nights extra interesting was the rise of a gang of slippery, sneaky burglars operating in the town. Besides, Silchar was grappling with severe power shortages and from 5 pm onward, we had power cuts every other hour, extending until 11 pm. And you know what? These power cuts turned out to be a gift from the electricity gods for these cunning thieves.

Their modus operandi was as peculiar as it was hilarious. While they were part of a well-organized gang, they never worked as a team. Each burglar fancied a solo act. As the power cuts swept over the town like clockwork, day after day they'd slink out to find their prey. If they spotted a house with an unlocked rear door, one of them would glide in, shedding their clothes down to the bare minimum – just the dark undies.

But wait, there's more. These guys weren't just any burglars; they were the professionals of the criminal world. They would apply their bodies with some odourless, super-slick oil, probably designed by Houdini himself. Once inside, they'd tiptoe around, grabbing clothes, cash, and valuables, whatever they could lay their hands on. Now, here's the pièce de résistance – they would make their great escape with the booty, but not without leaving one of their shoes or slippers near the gate of the house they just pillaged. It was like a visiting card of the fashionably challenged thief.

And this burglary extravaganza had two standout features. Firstly, the oily body and secondly the dark undie ensemble, because, you know, if caught, they could simply slip away. It happened to my colleague, KC, who lived nearby just a little away from my house. He had rented the first floor of a beautiful house made from wood with a slant roof- it was an elegant log house with shining floors and a green rooftop. The best part was the sprawling balcony all along the front – almost ten feet wide with a wooden railing overlooking the lawn and the road in the front. One frosty night, he heard a noise from the living room. He jumped out of his bed and as he sprang into action, he found himself wrestling a guy in his undies, coated in oil. And guess who ended up doing a floor routine? Yes, it was KC, as he pounced on the dark figure, he slipped and fell face down on the floor of his log house. The guy jumped to the ground floor from the balcony and escaped.

But that's not all. Another side-splitting incident starred a senior colleague, Mr. Sahay's son, the aspiring engineer. As he was preparing for entrance examinations, he was literally burning the midnight oil- studying till late in the night. One night Mr. Sahay got up hearing a strange 'thudd' sound past midnight and came out into the lobby of the house. He saw the light of his son's room on and asked, "Son are you studying this late" Pat came the enthusiastic reply, "Hmmm." Very pleased, Mr. Sahay went back to his room and slept. Little did he know that it was the burglar having a midnight tête-à-tête with him before swiping the house!

Next morning, he discovered that the house had been burgled. The thief had taken 2-3 suitcases out of his house, emptied them into a brand-new suitcase and left, leaving behind a left foot shoe next to the gate. Mr. Sahay asked his son whether he knew of anything because he was awake till past midnight but he told him that he had gone to sleep last night at 11 pm since he was very tired. It was the burglar who had replied to Mr. Sahay query that night!

The gang when nabbed by the local police, revealed two reasons for leaving behind a shoe or a slipper- it would be an indication for the gangmates on the prowl that the job's afoot and no need to waste time on the empty nest! The second reason they told was a real gem- they maintained that if they have taken away something they are also leaving behind something in return- this would overcome their guilt of committing a theft- *the guilt absolving strategy* indeed. Take something, leave something behind. Classic Robin Hood if you ask me!

The story doesn't end here. During their reign of slip-and-slide terror, we the residents of Silchar developed a new habit of locking our front and rear doors from the inside at night to prevent the entry or exit of an unwarranted visitor, if it so happens! Days passed but fate had other plans.

 One day early in the morning at around 4.30 am, we were jolted awake by a powerful earthquake. The ground was shaking as I grabbed our elder 5-year-old son in my arms and my wife picked up the younger one and we both rushed towards the front door to attempt a grand escape. But the door was locked from inside! In the panic we couldn't recollect where the keys were kept last night after locking it. I went back to the bedroom and my wife rushed to the dining room. We frantically searched for the keys, turning our house into an impromptu hide-and-seek arena but we couldn't locate the key. By this time the tremors had called it quits. Later we found that the keys were kept nowhere else but under my pillow. We then realised that locking the door from inside was not a wise decision not only for the sake of an earthquake but also for the crafty culprits, as the old saying goes- *even a cornered cat can jump back*. That day onwards we didn't lock our front door - *Life is worth more than the whole world- Jaan hai to jahan hai!*

From then on, we embraced the slippery mess with open arms. Because, well, Silchar was the town where in those days burglars oiled up, dropped shoes, and made burglary a hilarious art form – *and we didn't want to miss the show!*

Blessed House

It was the end of the year 1985 and all of us- the four brothers and a sister with our families were in Lucknow. My parents lived in Lucknow and my younger brother with his family also lived here with them. Often, we used to visit Lucknow for a family get-together. Our house was bustling with activity as the three generations were congregating here after a long time- lot of fun, enjoyment and merry making was ongoing almost round the clock. During one such enchanting evening, our parents called us for a meeting. Amongst other things my father told us that he had bought a piece of land measuring about 450 square yards in Dehradun from the housing board – the UP Avas Vikas Parishad (UPAVP).

He shared that the plot came with a catch: it was allotted to him as a civil service executive on the condition that construction on the land must commence before the fiscal year's end, lest it be forfeited by the government. The clock was ticking, with a mere three months left until the ominous deadline of March 31, 1986! Though this deadline was known to my parents from much before but the expectation was that this would be extended as had been happening for the past three years or so. Not wanting to keep this issue pending, they thought of asking all the five of us about our interest in this property. None of my siblings- sister who is the eldest and three brothers- two elder and one younger - were keen on settling down in the picturesque valley of Dehradun. Since I was posted in Dehradun and my company ONGC too was headquartered here, I offered to construct a house on this land out of a housing loan. As a welfare measure to its executives, ONGC among many such schemes, also offered housing loan at very competitive terms, repayable in manageable multiple monthly installments.

But, of course, every great endeavour comes with its challenges. The first hurdle was to secure the transfer of the land in my name from UPAVP, Dehradun. Simultaneously, I needed to navigate the maze of bureaucracy and gain approval for the house map blueprint from the Mussoorie Dehradun Development Authority (MDDA). It was indeed a complex dance between paperwork and deadlines. My father assured me of the plot's transfer in my name within a month's time. He rang up the UPAVP Chief, a young civil services officer and put in a word with him about his decision to pass on the plot to me. With determination in my heart and the support of my family, I embarked on this adventure. On my return to Dehradun, I met him- a very helpful soul who got the process rolled out that very day and within a month and a half, the plot was transferred in my name.

In the race against time to find an architect for my dream home, I hit a dead end- couldn't find one in such a short time. However, I found a couple of manuals on home architecture in my Institute's library, got them issued, studied these, and decided to draw the construction map of the house on my own. I could finish this job in 10-15 days flat, approached an architect and got it countersigned by him by paying his fee which was Rs. 500 in those days. Paid another Rs. 75 to get 3 blueprints of the drawing. I submitted the application to the Development Authority -MDDA for approval of my map. Luckily the concerned Junior Engineer (JE) turned out to be a youngster and a very friendly guy. When he heard my dilemma of running against the deadline of 31st, he genuinely helped me a lot by pushing my case hard. Miraculously, he secured all the necessary approvals but the final one within a month. On day the final approval was expected, I reached his office in the evening but he looked a little perturbed when I met him. He placed the file before me, the final authority had thrown in a spanner- a query, which he told was unwarranted in UPAVP cases. He lamented that had he been personally present, he could have explained this to the approving authority but now this would take time and meant that I may miss the UPAVP deadline. I remembered the old proverb- *Man proposes God disposes*!

Anyway, I was thinking of approaching UPAVP the next working day and request a week's extension after giving proof of *'work in progress'* on map approval process. But just then it so happened that the JE who was refilling his ink pen from the ink pot, inadvertently hit the pot which fell over the open file and the ink spread all over the *noting* on that page. Seeing this, I almost panicked but he did not, he rather smiled. The file was left over the weekend to dry up and the next working day he carried it to the concerned authority, explained to him the case and got the approval on a fresh note as the previous noting was masked under the spilled ink! Was this circus played by the inkpot orchestrated by the unassuming JE intentionally or was it an intervention of divine forces - I could never understand.

The rest of the job was rather easy. I got a housing loan from ONGC and gave the construction contract to a contractor known through a close acquaintance. I had to do the usual running around to arrange the construction material, deodar wood, statutory approvals for water, sewerage and electrical connections, the electrical, sanitary and plumbing material and wood work fittings and fixtures, etc. etc. the list was long. Getting the house loan installments released in a timely manner, keeping a tab on the contractor and the material being consumed and a thorough two stage termite treatment since the plot had a huge anthill. All this I could manage before and after office hours on a day-to-day basis. Finally, the construction was completed with whitewash and painting jobs done by March, 1987. This was followed by a house-warming party in April on the Baisakhi day.

It was an East facing land with a 30' wide road in front lined up by the regal Jakaranda trees on the two sides with their remarkable purple bloom. Ascend to the rooftop, and you'd be greeted by a breathtaking view of the majestic Mussoorie ranges. We had a lawn in the front and a decent sized kitchen garden at the back. The priest who came for the Pooja did tell me that the house was auspicious from all the aspects but little did I know that fate had something extraordinary in store! Little did we realize that this house would become a repository of interesting stories, laughter and benedictions.

Since my wife is in the teaching profession, we preferred to continue to stay in our official residence in the ONGC Campus for safety's sake.

Dehradun has been infamous for daytime burglaries and since we were just the two of us, we decided not to shift but rather let this new house be out for rent. I kept this house till 2011 and in this period of 24 years we saw 4 tenants- each with an interesting tale.

The first tenants were a family of five. The husband was a civil engineer, the wife and three daughters- eldest being in standard X. A very nice family. During a conversation with them, we came to know that they were looking forward to a male child in the family since they held the view that a family is not complete unless the offspring are from both genders!

Sacred Beginnings: Crafting the Future Home

My wife and I had tied the knot just a few years ago and we hadn't really delved into such matters. We were still navigating the intricacies of matching the curtains! So, we kept smiling and nodding to what they said. We didn't visit them much because both of us were working and used to be busy with family and friends and more so, we have always been non-interfering house-owners so long as the rent is being deposited, regularly. During a visit on the New Year, we noticed a newborn baby in the house- a baby boy! They both were beaming with joy as they broke the news of this new arrival to us. For nearly six years, they inhabited our humble abode, turning it into their haven - a hassle-free stay with absolutely no problems.

Ready to Dwell- the Mystic Home

The next tenant was a colleague from ONGC, a sweet couple, married for nearly two years and were nice company. We exchanged visits with them a few times till we were in Dehradun. The conversation revolved around lot many things of our common interests including children. By this time, we had our first child, a baby boy- a November 1987 edition and baby number two was enroute! They were keen on a girl child, especially the hubby who held a fervent desire for a girl child. He used to be rather poetic about the virtues of daughters, convinced that they were the epitome of affection, sincerity, and care- rightly so.

Anyway, we moved to Silchar in the latter half of 1990 with our two children. A visit back to Dehradun in the summer of the following year unfolded a heartwarming surprise. I visited my house and the gentleman gleefully shared that his wife was with her parents as they were blessed with baby-girl about a month back! Naturally, they were very happy. Evidently, joy had found a new address. They lived in our house for over four years, then moved to Mumbai on posting.

Our third act in the tenant chronicles starred a middle-aged executive with two daughters, one doing her graduation and the other in high school. Hailing from the halls of tradition, this family firmly believed in the archaic notion that a dynasty's continuity hinged on the existence of a male heir.

Everyone is entitled to his own views, I thought, and wished them luck and a blessed life. This gentleman was a maestro in the art of meticulousness and would religiously deposit the monthly rent by 7th day of the month deducting whatever he spent on routine maintenance. To add a dash of drama, he even took from me 11 self-addressed, stamped envelopes wherein he would regularly send me a copy of the Bank's pay-in slip of the rent and the receipts of maintenance done- sometimes even a tap washer costing Rs. 2 and another Rs 20 as the plumber's labour charges! Very thorough indeed, he was the Sherlock Holmes of rent payments and maintenance procedures.

The plot thickened when, one day, a letter arrived bearing news of a grand plan—he had decided to get a Mexican grass lawn laid out in our house. He graciously informed me that Rs. 800 would be deducted from the coming month's rent for this purpose. In a moment of landlordly wisdom, I wrote a courteous reply, politely informing him that while I admired his enthusiasm for the Mexican grass, the financial responsibility fell squarely on his shoulders. I further wrote that since it's the tenant's prerogative to have a lawn or a kitchen garden of his choice he only has to bear the cost and not the house-owner. He replied instantly saying that since he was on a transferable job and couldn't have carried the lawn with him when transferred, the house owner must bear the cost. He also very generously granted me a discount of Rs. 200 as a good gesture on his part and deducted Rs. 600 from next month's rent! One of the later days, in one of his letters on my self-addressed stamped envelope he also informed me of the good news of them being blessed with a baby boy. I felt happy for him. Their tenure in our house was a rollercoaster of surprises, meticulous accounts, and a touch of horticultural drama. Almost six years later, they bid our house farewell.

Lastly, the fourth tenant in the house was a defense personnel, a young couple who didn't have children till then. In fact, I always preferred ONGCians for letting out my house but as the luck would have it, in the early 2000s ONGC offices in Dehradun were bereft of executives and I too was posted in Baroda hence it was very difficult to get ONGCians as tenants. Defense personnel are also a landlord's dream tenant since most move on postings within three years in a clockwork manner and in general their dealings are as crisp and precise as a military salute. However, in a twist that I never could imagine, these tenants shattered the mold. Instead of the usual three-year stint, this guy secured a lien with the state government, deciding to set roots in our house for an extended run. Intriguingly, this couple too was particular about their progeny and were finally blessed with a baby of their choice!

Unfortunately, the time came when I had to bid adieu to this haven of happiness. I had to sell off this house since we had plans to settle elsewhere after my superannuation. Such a blessed house indeed, it made everyone happy- fulfilling their wishes of a lifetime! It had positive vibes and turned out to be a sacred dwelling for its occupants who enjoyed happiness, success and abundance. There weren't any Vaastu concepts in those days, it was only the *Havan* we had organized under the blessings of our parents and siblings who had

My father and nephews just before housewarming ceremony

attended the ceremony along with close family friends.

Today, I find myself avoiding the road where this fascinating house once stood— the new owner decided to demolish it.

A house that was once a beacon of joy, spreading happiness and charm, now lay in ruins, obscured beneath thick unruly vegetation. It's a haunting sight, and I can't help but feel a pinch of sadness at the fate of a place that held so many memories.

But amidst the rubble, the foundation of that blessed house stands tall, a silent testament to the joy it once housed. The echoes of laughter and the whispers of dreams linger in the air, proving that even though the physical structure may be gone, the spirit of a truly magical home lives on.......

Godsend

This is a tale from June 2005 during our Baroda days. I was speeding back to Baroda on the newly constructed Ahmedabad-Baroda Expressway with my teenaged son and his friend. I had taken them both to Ahmedabad for their All-India Engineering Entrance Examination. The road was excellent and deserted, so I was doing over 130 KMPH in my Maruti Esteem. We were almost half-way, just 5 km short of Nadiad when I realized that the car was pulling heavily towards the left side. Suspecting something amiss, I pulled over to the left and brought the car to a halt on the bay area- yes it was a flat tyre. Incidentally, it so happened that the spare wheel too was flat!

I immediately rang up the E-way emergency service for help. They promptly reverted saying that they would be there within an hour with a recovery van since one recovery van each used to be parked on each side of the E-way. Considering the fact that the front of the car is always heavier because of the engine, we removed one of the rear wheels, placed it in the front and kept the rear wheel with the flat tyre. I told the boys to sit huddled up in the front passenger seat and started driving slowly with the idea to reach Nadiad and look for a repair shop.

We had barely reached the overhead bridge of Nadiad when the rear tyre which was flat already got torn to shreds and the car came to a halt. Being an E-way, that too very new and now at 6.30 pm in the evening, there wasn't a single soul around what to say of a repair shop. Only the cars and trucks were zipping past at very high speed. We had no option but to wait here for the recovery van.

I was cursing myself for not checking the spare wheel before taking up the journey in the morning. Normally, I am very particular with my detailed checklist before performing any journey- tool kit, first aid kit, jack and spare wheel but probably I took this trip too lightly being a short distance one. While engrossed in these thoughts, I noticed a man standing on the overhead bridge waving at us. My son went to him and the gentleman asked him what the problem was. On listening to my son, he offered to help and told my son to bring the flat tyre up on the overbridge and that he would take him to a nearby tyre repair shop. Since the wheel was quite heavy and would become heavier once repaired, both the boys decided to go together. They took the wheel down the parapetted E-way and then up the overbridge through the flight of over 75 steps and vanished from my sight.

I waited and waited – the boys were nowhere to be seen for the next 30 minutes. It was dark by then. I was getting anxious and fidgety since they had gone with a stranger. I was thinking that I too could have accompanied them. Immersed in these thoughts, I was planning to go after them when my mobile phone rang up- it was my son calling from an unknown number. He said that the wheel had two punctures, hence the delay and that they were with the gentleman at his house enjoying cold drinks and snacks. Both the boys appeared back in another 15 minutes and carefully brought down the wheel. As we were replacing the wheel, the recovery van also arrived. We paid the dues and thanked the recovery van guys and started driving back home.

My son told me that the gentleman – Manish, who helped us was an engineering graduate and son of a big businessman of Nadiad. While the boys were with him and they came to know that the repair will take about half an hour, Manish took them to his house which was nearby. There he shared his story with them. He had got married just six months back from this very house. One fateful evening, he set off with his bride for a long joyride in his car on the expansive E-way. As they traced their way back home around the sunset time, tragedy struck—the car spiralled out of control, colliding beneath an overpass in a horrific accident. They both were unconscious for some time. When Manish regained consciousness, he somehow wriggled out of the wreckage of the car and tried signalling down the cars asking for help. He and his wife were badly injured. He kept crying for help but not a single soul stopped and finally when the aid arrived it was too late. His newly wedded wife succumbed to the injuries. He was in the hospital for two weeks before he could recover from his fractured ribs and other injuries. He was full of remorse that he couldn't save his wife.

Once healed, he chose to dedicate an hour each evening to the same overpass that witnessed their dreams shatter to help people travelling on E-way who were in some kind of distress. Almost half an hour since, we were now entering Baroda when my

The Nadiad Overbridge seen at a distance

mobile phone rang up, I slowed down and answered the call.

It was Manish, he asked me, "Have you reached back safely. I am still here on the overbridge and I thought to ask you about your journey back home before I leave for my home." His kindness for strangers, for us, touched a chord deep within me. With gratitude echoing in my voice, I responded, "Thanks a ton, Manish. You were our unexpected savior today. God bless you."

Pat came the reply, *"Not at all, Sir. I am an Indian and this is the bare minimum that an Indian can do for a fellow-Indian when in need."* Though I never met Manish, either then or ever after but my heart always fills up with gratitude and pride for such fellow Indians. A big salute to Manish!

A Tryst with Gypsy Girls

It was September the 5, 2005, I was having lunch at my home during lunch hour in Baroda when my phone rang heralding a significant turn of events. The call emanated from the New Delhi office of the newly appointed Director of Exploration at ONGC. With curiosity in his voice, he inquired about my whereabouts. Little did I know that this conversation would alter the course of my professional journey. As the dialogue unfolded and I told him that I was at my residence for lunch, he equipped, "you can enjoy this luxury for another 8-9 days because you are now moving to New Delhi and need to report by 15th September." On my query about my posting in New Delhi, he casually mentioned the establishment of a new Centre of Excellence, where I would assume the leadership role of heading the International Desk. I had no option but to comply.

On reaching New Delhi, I came to know that the International Desk had a crack team of 11 hand-picked geoscientists, and I was selected to Head it because of my recent international exposure on my posting in Sudan. Including me, we were 12 of us to help ONGC's overseas arm ONGC Videsh Limited (OVL) in its due diligence of Mergers & Acquisition activities and evaluation of drilling proposals from existing overseas assets- some in OVL called us *the dirty dozen*- after the popular Hollywood movie of the sixties! Our task was clear – navigate the intricacies of international exploration and contribute to ONGC's global ventures.

My first overseas assignment was to lead a multi-disciplinary team of ten executives to the ENI- the Italian National Oil Company- headquarters in Milan to study their offer of oil/gas blocks for proposed partnering with OVL and in return ENI was to study blocks offered by ONGC in India. It was a 5-day visit and we reached Milan via Vienna on a Sunday morning by an Air Austria flight. The ENI office was in San Donato suburb about 10 Kms southeast of Milan City where we stayed in a cozy and comfortable Hotel recommended by the ENI counterparts.

Whether on an official or a personal overseas visit, I normally make it a point to carry the address and contact details of the local Embassy, High Commission or the Consulate as the case may be, and on the first available opportunity inform them about my/our arrival in that City. This practice has been ingrained in me through the experiences of acquaintances who found themselves in need of assistance in foreign lands. I firmly believe that proactively reaching out to our diplomats creates a positive rapport, and in the unlikely event of needing help or support, it becomes readily forthcoming.

Fortunately, in my extensive travel history comprising multiple overseas trips, I have never found myself in a situation requiring such assistance. And there was only one instance where an Indian Ambassador couldn't accommodate a meeting due to prior commitments. Otherwise, my interactions with these diplomatic representatives have been overwhelmingly positive. They typically extend a warm welcome and express satisfaction when visitors like me make a courtesy call or drop by.

In keeping with this tradition, I requested my colleague and friend Randeep to contact the Indian Consulate after our kick-off meeting with the Italians on following Monday. We were given a time of 12 noon the next day. Randeep and I reached the Consulate at the appointed hour. The Counsellor General Mr. Kapoor welcomed the two of us in his office. A fine gentleman, inquisitive about our objective of visiting the ENI, he discussed details about India's energy security and offered to help in whatever way he could.

He gave us quite a few tips on do's and don'ts in Italy. He cautioned us to be careful about cash and documents while walking in crowded places or in public transport. He was very categorical in telling us that the foreigners especially non-Europeans get recognized simply by their body language and become easy targets of the pickpockets. We sat with him for about 45 minutes and took his leave at around 12:45 pm. We walked out of the plush Consulate Office in Milan city centre, amused but conscious. It seemed that everyone was following us! As we signalled down a Cab and dashed back to the ENI offices, little did we know what was lying in store for us.

Since it was already fifteen minutes past 1 o'clock in the afternoon, we got dropped outside the ENI office at San Donato and decided to walk down to McDonalds which was less than half a kilometer from this place. We had an option to have lunch in the office cafeteria like all the local staff and executives but all of us- the visiting Indians wanted to try out Mc Donald. Behind the ENI office, there was a filling station facing the Expressway and alongside was a lonely stretch of road that led to McDonalds.

As we entered this stretch bypassing the filling station, admiring the grand expressway to our left and the forest to our right, suddenly two girls jumped out of the woods and blocked our way. We were a little surprised at this, although we had seen these girls last evening too, pleading for cigarettes when a few of us were passing through a park near our hotel. They looked like Romani girls also popularly called gypsies- one must have been in her early twenties and the other in late twenties with a baby wrapped in a shawl in one of her hands. Both the girls were brunettes with well chiselled facial features. Last evening, they followed us demanding cigarettes, repeatedly saying 'sigarretano, sigarretano' till we got out of the park.

Suddenly, the older one accosted me and tried to put her hand in the inner pocket of my business suit's jacket. I instantly yelled at her and forcefully pushed her away. She was about to fall but balanced herself as she came on her knees. Once free, I ran a few steps then started walking briskly towards McDonalds. This is probably what they wanted. The moment I was away, they both clung to Randeep, held him on to both his hands and started frisking him. As he cried for help, I turned back and was horrified to witness the unsettling sight- Randeep trying to run but his raiders, running alongside, had gripped him hard romping all over him putting their hands in his pockets looking for valuables and money.

I suddenly noticed that, in the melee, something fell out of Randeep's pocket but none of them noticed as they were all running. I immediately started walking back towards them and as I neared them, the two girls tried to drag him towards the other side of the road. Meanwhile, I had seen that what fell out of Randeep's pocket was a bundle of Euros rolled up and held by a rubber band. They were the same Euros which he had got encashed in exchange for the travellers' cheques in the morning from a Bank near our Hotel. So, I hurried past them and before the girls could see or understand anything, I pounced on the roll, picked it up and held tightly onto my clenched fist. They had seen me picking up something, but before they could do anything, Randeep succeeded in freeing himself from them. Luckily for us, at that very moment, an SUV drove down from behind. Seeing the commotion on the road, the SUV driver stopped over and started honking, repeatedly. Now Randeep and I both got a chance to run towards McDonalds.

We thanked the SUV guy and as he sped away, we saw that our raiders were still standing on the other side of road at a distance nonchalantly, giving flying kisses and calling us back gesturing with their index finger. We kept on walking fast and stopped only when we were inside the restaurant's premises.

Randeep had a sigh of relief when I told him that his Euros were intact! Our hearts still pounding, we waited outside for a while to have fresh air and bring down our heartbeats to normal level before joining our friends for lunch leaving behind the tumultuous encounter on the expressway.

I checked on the internet later, it's a common practice with these girls- the baby that they carry is more than often a doll to distract the unsuspecting tourist. They generally operate as a two-some, one would distract the victim by engaging him/her in conversation holding a hand and the other would pick the pocket. If caught, they very swiftly run away. I came across a news article in the Washington Post of July 2000 about Ben Johnson being robbed in Rome of about US$ 4500.

It was amusing to note that the world record holder of his times in the 100-metre dash, couldn't catch his tormentor- a suspected Romani woman! Johnson was distracted with pleas for money by a girl while her accomplice, a woman picked his pocket and took off with his wallet. He caught the girl, but the woman got away! She had a 15-second start on Johnson. It was the same modus operandi that they used on him. The girl held his hand, and the woman picked the pocket.

Before leaving Milan on Saturday, I rang up Mr. Kapoor and thanked him once again for his timely advice that had alerted us and largely prevented the broad daylight robbery attempt of these two lurking girls becoming successful!

Mysterious Midnight Call

The winter of year 2006 was as smoggy as it used to be every year in New Delhi. The crop residue burning in adjacent western states, the overcrowded streets with thousands of vehicles of all sizes and shapes billowing smoke, the rising dust from never-ending construction, the jet fuel emissions from hundreds of jets crisscrossing in the skies, all mixed with the moist and heavy December air makes the Capital City a smoke chamber. Driving under such conditions becomes a real challenge, especially during late evenings and nights when the visibility drops to a mere few meters.

No matter how difficult and how unsafe it becomes to drive but the indomitable spirit of Delhiites cannot be crushed during this time which actually is an extended festive season in India. New Year and Christmas celebrations are in full swing with frequent get-togethers which extend late into the nights.

My wife and I had returned from one such rendezvous late in the night, parked our car in the designated lot, climbed up to our second-floor apartment in Vasant Kunj and hit the sack. Past midnight, I was woken up from my deep sleep by a call on my mobile phone. Cursing the caller, I looked for my phone kept on the side table and tried to see who it was at this hour. I couldn't believe my eyes and I got up with a tremble and sat up in my bed staring at the phone screen. To my horror, it was a call from my own landline phone. The landline phone was in the room next to the lobby in our three-bedroom apartment. Neither of the two children were with us during those days and we were just the two of us in the house, in our bedroom. I rubbed my eyes multiple times to ensure that I was correctly reading the screen which displayed the caller as *'Self Home LL'*! LL meant landline. I wasn't able figure it out that how could someone enter a house properly locked from inside and then ring me up on my mobile phone from my landline. To me it didn't make sense but I was faced with this situation.

This house was a second-floor apartment with three doors- one for the main entrance and one each for the front and rear balconies. The house owner had got the iron grill doors fitted on all these three locations as an added security measure. Even the windows had strong iron grills. Since we were a working couple and used to be away from home all through the day, we were very particular to securely latch and lock the doors from outside. The same drill was repeated in the night before sleeping every night from the inside. Hence, there wasn't any chance of a lapse on our side of leaving any of the three doors unlocked. These thoughts were flashing across my mind in quick succession but the mobile phone kept ringing.

I woke up my wife who was fast asleep. It took her a few moments to realize what was happening. When she woke up fully and the seriousness of the situation sank in, she too was perturbed with her eyes wide open in disbelief. Meanwhile, I took the call and said "Hello" once, twice, and thrice but there wasn't any answer. I disconnected the call and dialed my landline number but it was continuously busy. We were in a strange situation. Could it really be a burglar who somehow got trapped inside and wanted to get out? But then why call, why not knock on the door to confront us for the keys or open one of the doors to escape. Removing the curtain, I looked out of the window - it was pitch dark outside because of dense fog or smog or whatever. Only a small halo around the streetlights could be seen. The flight of imagination was soaring high- at that moment, the thought of this being an eerie encounter crossed my mind and left me with a frightening chill.

We quickly discussed between the two of us in a hushed tone and made up a strategy to salvage the situation. As planned my wife rang up our next-door neighbours, apologized to them for calling up at an odd hour and explained to them the entire situation. It took several minutes for them also to digest the situation. They agreed to call up another couple staying upstairs and be ready outside our main door to face any eventuality together- friendly neighbours indeed!

My wife had no. 100 punched on her mobile and ready to press 'call', if needed. I then picked up a golf club from my golf set kept in one corner of the bedroom and unbolted our bedroom door moving stealthily and cautiously not making any noise. I opened the door slowly and switched on the lobby lights which were just outside the bedroom door. Meanwhile, once the lights were on, my wife dashed straight to the entrance door to open it. I bolted to the adjacent room where the landline instrument was kept but there was total silence and no activity. However, the phone receiver was off the cradle but no one was around. I then quickly checked the rest of the house but couldn't find anyone.

I came back to the place where the landline phone was kept. I noticed that in addition to the receiver being off the cradle, some milk was also spilled over the phone from a glass which had fallen on the phone cabinet. By this time, our good neighbours armed with a baseball bat and a cricket wicket were already there and checking every nook and corner of the house. We checked the rooms, wardrobes, below the beds, kitchen shelves, toilets and finally the storeroom.

Lo and behold, to our surprise, we discovered a cat curled up on a rug kept in one corner of our storeroom. The little fellow with dark stripes was staring at us with a rather scared look in her light green eyes. On seeing so many humans around her, she was trying to withdraw further into herself, making her curl tighter with a meek meoww..... The culprit was found! It was the cat that I had often observed perched on a wall or darting down a tree in the neighborhood.

What next? Now the six heads put together, inferred the likely sequence of events- the cat must have got trapped inside the house during the day through the rear balcony door which often remained open.

At night on our return from the party, I had a glass of milk and left the glass on the telephone cabinet while checking for any missed calls during our absence. Once we were off to sleep, the poor cat climbed up the cabinet and tried to have the leftover milk. It spilled the milk over the phone and

in the process the phone receiver also came off the cradle. While slurping the milk with her tongue, the redial button was pressed accidentally which started the entire scary scene! I checked the redial record of that evening, my wife had called me that evening on my mobile to enquire about the evening's programme.

The mystery was solved! And all the six of us said in a chorus- "It's elementary, my dear Watson!"

Aerial Odyssey- On a Whirlybird to Doon Valley

It was a sultry August morning during 2008 in New Delhi and there I stood in the lounge of the Indira Gandhi International Airport, New Delhi awaiting my boarding call for a chopper bound for Dehradun. The twist in the tale had begun the previous evening at around six when my boss called me up. He conveyed that I along with another colleague needed to accompany him on an impromptu journey to Dehradun for a crucial business meeting scheduled for 9:30 am the next day. His personal staff had already informed him that the night train tickets were not available and the journey by road would be a little tricky because of the prevailing flood situation on the way- road conditions weren't good. Going by helicopter was thought to be the most pragmatic option.

This was to be my first ever ride by chopper, so I was game for a new kind of experience and adventure. This is despite knowing that our chopper was of an old vintage but the excitement was at its peak. The motto has always been '*duty is duty*' and it needs to be performed when called for by whatever means available with full vigour and enthusiasm!

Without a moment's hesitation, I dialed up my colleague, who sat just a room away and together we launched the preparation for the meeting on the horizon. Accustomed to burning the midnight oil due to work pressure, we wrapped up our work in the late hours that day too at almost 10 pm and were at the airport at 7.30 am in the morning. The stage was set for a day that promised not just the meeting but an exciting chopper ride into the unknown!

The boarding formalities took another half an hour and we were ready to board the flying machine at 8 am. It was an eight-seater chopper with two pilots, a flight engineer and the three of us, the passengers. The moment we entered, we were greeted with a flurry of instructions- fasten your seat belts and equip yourselves with oversized headsets, a curious blend of earphones and a microphone. All the crew members were in their respective seats, ready to take off. I was snugly sitting immediately behind the two pilots in the aisle seat, my boss on the far end window seat and my colleague on the second row with the flight engineer. The pilot was an elderly man with silvery white hair, a well-trimmed white beard and a personality that exuded confidence even in the most nervous of the passengers. His eyes bore the wisdom of thousands of hours spent navigating the boundless skies. On the contrary, the co-pilot, a youngster probably in his late twenties, displayed a casual attitude, in stark contrast to the seasoned veteran by his side.

 As the twin engines started and the throttle gained momentum, the chopper started vibrating and shaking severely with a lot of noise. The rattle reminded me of the age-old Leyland DTC buses of the eighties- once I had to travel to Dehradun from Delhi in one such bus sitting on a seat next to the bonnet! Same was the feeling today. With the chopper blades now rotating at full speed, the machine lifted in the air for about 50 feet then suddenly nose-dived and took off in the air. The abrupt maneuver caught me off guard and for a fleeting moment my heart was almost in my mouth!

Rapidly gaining altitude in a northwesterly direction, we soared in the high skies and a mysterious dark patch of clouds engulfed us after about 15-20 minutes. Visibility plummeted to zero, yet the chopper effortlessly navigated through the ominous clouds. In another minute, there was condensation inside the chopper and water droplets started falling on the two control panels located between the two pilots. I was becoming anxious as these two control panels belonged to the two engines and water could result in a short-circuit or something like that, I thought.

As I was in the grip of these disturbing thoughts, the co-pilot sprang into action- opened the glove compartment on his front and fetched two white towel rolls. He, very skillfully, draped them protectively on each of the two control panels! The pilot looked at him approvingly and gave him a thumbs up which he promptly acknowledged with a similar gesture. I also had a sigh of relief, realizing that condensation on the control panel is a normal thing and that's why they had kept the towel rolls ready to be draped on the panels!

Flying ahead, we came out of the bad weather patch in a while and now a clear bright sky was visible in the front with patches of white clouds here and there. The flight was now becoming enjoyable because of the good visibility and a spectacular view of the settlements, cities and fields down below. The chopper was gaining more height as the pilot was continuously rotating the multiple knobs on the two control panels now that the towels were removed by the junior. Observing him from behind, I gathered that he was trying to keep both the engines in equivalence of speed, torque, frequency, efficiency, etc.

Everything looked good when at one point in time, the co-pilot quickly reversed the changes that the pilot had made. The pilot looked at the co-pilot for a moment and again brought back the controls to their original positions. Undeterred, the youngster attempted to tinker with the controls once again looking at his senior disapprovingly. But the veteran pilot intervened, signaling a firm 'no' with a raised forefinger, his gaze unwavering. Unfazed, the co-pilot muttered something into his microphone, getting a response from the pilot to fetch, probably the SOP Manual (Standard Operating Procedure), from the glove compartment.

In a comical turn of events, the co-pilot retrieved the hefty manual and started diligently scanning through the contents page. Meanwhile, the pilot took the manual in his hand and opened the relevant page and gave it back to his junior and gestured to him to read the procedure at that page. It was clear that the pilot remembered it by heart. The co-pilot read the procedure for a while and gave a thumbs up to the Pilot, bowed his head in gratification to his senior and settled in his seat now relaxed. And so, I too felt relaxed after this quite an amusing situation!

In another 20 minutes we reached our destination. Our return journey was scheduled in the late afternoon again by the same chopper and the crew, after the meeting. Considering this morning's escapade, I told my resourceful office assistant to see if a seat was up for grabs on the evening train under the *'tatkal scheme'* and I did get one. It promised a contrasting journey – tracks beneath instead of clouds above!

Rubbing Shoulders

I was casually scrolling through my emails after lunch when, out of nowhere, Virendra, a colleague from my team (name changed), burst into the room. He wore an expression of shock and distress, as if he had just encountered a ghost. As he sat before me dramatically placing his hands on his head, he looked like the embodiment of despair.

This happened nearly one-and-a-half decades ago. I was then leading a team of management services group, a squad of extremely efficient executives with excellent managerial and technical traits. Virendra was one of them. I offered him a glass of water and asked about the calamity that had befallen him.

And so, begins the hilarious tale of errors due to flawed misunderstandings. That day, Virendra was to leave on a long vacation with his wife and he had left the office early. He could barely reach his home with vacation dreams in his eyes when he got a call from the Chief's office. He was summoned back from his freedom. The moment he entered the office he was bombarded with multiple queries and a serious allegation by the Chief who was furious and enraged. The accusation? Virendra apparently had an indecent misadventure at a recent wedding. It was indeed scandalous, shocking and shameful!

Virendra vehemently denied having been involved in any such incident. He explained that he was just doing his duty at the wedding as requested by the host. He and his wife were requested to look after the VIPs, making sure the senior officials and accompanying spouses at the wedding were treated like royalty. But the Chief wasn't convinced and told that his behavior had tarnished the company's image and he will now have to face the consequences- he may even be shunted out on transfer to some other place.

Not convinced, Virendra pressed for details and he was directed to a company executive who had played the whistleblower. Virendra, hot on the trail of the gossipy whistleblower, finally found him sitting pretty in his office room. When confronted, he claimed that a couple of officials told him about Virendra's escapades of inappropriately touching the guests while offering plates to them during dinner at the wedding. To make things worse he further claimed that those people were smiling as they gossiped about Virendra's so-called dinner escapades. As Virendra couldn't believe his ears, he didn't know how to react to this nonsensical rumour being spread against him.

Feeling dejected and desperate, Virendra poured his heart out to me, insisting it was all lies. I knew him well, as a cheerful and vibrant executive who wouldn't even think of such wrongful conduct. I immediately knew that there was some misunderstanding and I wanted to get to the bottom of it, after all Virendra was a part of my team.

I advised him to calm down, ring up the guy and ask him to narrate verbatim what was he told by those two gossipy officials whom he was quoting. Phone on speaker mode, we braced ourselves for the details and that's when it happened. The poor guy confessed that the grapevine buzzing about Virendra was serious and that these two officials said, "Hey, your friend Virendra was in high spirits at the dinner that night and was seen rubbing shoulders with the Chief Guest's wife and her friends."

As we hung up the phone, laughter erupted uncontrollably. The poor fellow, unfamiliar with the idiom 'rubbing shoulders,' inadvertently reported to the Chief, conveying that Virendra had engaged in inappropriate touching while in high spirits! 'Rubbing shoulders' simply means meeting or spending time with someone important or famous. Without wasting another moment, Virendra dashed to the Chief's office to narrate the comically misunderstood situation. We breathed a sigh of relief.

The power of workplace idioms should never be underestimated, especially when someone's reputation is on the line!

Frosty Wings at Heathrow

During the year 2011, my professional journey took an exhilarating turn as I assumed the role in the company's overseas arm in bustling heart of New Delhi. Leading a dynamic team of around fifteen executives, our mission was as expansive as it was crucial – to steer the ship of business development for the company.

The role involved scouting and screening of suitable overseas oil/gas opportunities globally and carrying out the required *due diligence* for a possible acquisition. The company was mandated by the Government to acquire overseas oil and gas assets in aid of energy security of the Nation. The nature of our mission meant frequent sojourns across the globe to carry out the *due diligence* of the offers on the table and often deal negotiations. It was a choreography of strategy, diligence, and compliance, transforming the M&A process into a symphony of precision and expertise.

We were on one such business trip to London during 2012. After the final round of negotiations with the sell-side during this visit, we boarded the afternoon flight to New Delhi from Heathrow

Airport. The flight on a Boeing 737 was to take off at 2.30 pm. The four of us travelling together were somewhat weary because of hectic negotiation rounds which lasted over long hours every day consecutively for the last three days punctuated with breakout meetings. That morning also, we had made an early checkout to reach the airport after attending to a pending issue on the way. As we settled in our seats in the aircraft, I dozed off even before the plane took off.

A gentle nudge interrupted my deep slumber and I found the suave flight purser standing beside me, a lunch tray already gracing my seat's table. Still sleepy, I asked him how long ago we took off. With a chuckle, he motioned me to look out of the windowpane. To my surprise, I realized that we were nestled quietly in a cozy corner of the parking bay. The purser unravelled the mystery, revealing that the plane hadn't actually taken off. It was in the midst of taxiing to the runway when the pilot detected a glitch with the 'de-icing' indicator—a crucial system ensuring flight safety. In the complex world of aviation, de-icing is a vital ritual, especially for larger airplanes. It prevents the perilous buildup of frost and ice on wings, windshields, and other critical parts during high-altitude flights. Left unaddressed, this icy encroachment could spell disaster by hampering flight performance. Large commercial aircraft come equipped with in-flight ice protection systems, designed to shed accumulated ice and thwart its resurgence. Realizing the non-functional state of this essential control component, the vigilant pilot made the call to bring the plane back to the parking bay for a thorough examination and prompt rectification. I thanked the purser for educating me with his endless wisdom on the ins and outs of this crucial flying gizmo. I never knew aircraft parts could be this entertaining!

Our journey, it seemed, was momentarily grounded due to the airline's unyielding commitment to passenger safety and rightly so. The flight purser-bearer of both news and food, added another layer to this unfolding tale. With a minimum of an hour's wait before liftoff, and the clock already striking 3:30 pm, he decided it was prudent to wake us up from our *mid-air* siesta for lunch.

The clock ticked away and at 5 pm, the pilot's voice crackled over the cabin's PA system, delivering news that a vital component required replacement and British Airways (BA) had been contacted with a plea to spare one from their inventory. Swiftly, the flight purser returned, becoming the harbinger of details. He revealed that the culprit was not the de-icing control indicator on the pilot's dashboard, as initially thought, but rather the de-icing sensor itself. It needed to be replaced. If BA had the required part, a mere hour stood between us and resuming our journey. The sensor panel, already open, will not take much time for replacement. We waited and waited in the hope of a resumption of the flight at any moment.

The pilot's voice returned at 6:30 pm, this time to deliver a different verdict. Despite the effort, BA couldn't find the elusive part in their inventory. The replacement would be ferried in by the early morning flight from India. He continued that the travel was arranged for the five first-class travellers on a Jet Airways flight departing for New Delhi within an hour. However, for the rest of us in the Business and Economy classes, a night at a Heathrow hotel awaited. He said that the delayed flight was estimated to resume its course at 10 am the next morning. Our routine journey had now transformed into an impromptu overnight layover at the crossroads of anticipation and uncertainty.

We were packed up in a few buses and taken to Hotel Ibis(?) nearby, just about 15 minutes' drive. Our luggage wasn't given to us on the logic that off-loading and loading again in the morning would take a lot of time. Few passengers showed concerns about their essential medicines and the shaving/dental kits but the airline authorities assured that the shaving/dental kits will be provided at the Hotel and a general practitioner will visit the Hotel right away to dispense with essential medicines for hypertension, diabetes, etc. to the needy. On arriving at the Hotel, we were allotted decent rooms but the mini bars were empty and there weren't any shaving or dental kits. The Hotel management told us to get these items from the vending machines placed in the lobby against payment!

Anyway, these are minor things looking at the fact that the alert pilot had detected the issue in a timely manner and saved what could have been a mid-air disaster. The hotel provided us with a buffet dinner which had a limited spread that could have been managed within a short time for over 100 passengers. Overall, the hotel stay was as comfortable as could be in a 3-star hotel.

The airlines staff had told us that the buses would arrive in the morning at 9 am and that we should be ready after checking out by then. All of us had our breakfast early and had queued up for check out around 9 am but there weren't any buses or airlines staff to be seen on the premises. At 10 am the Hotel staff told us to remove our luggage – mostly hand baggage from our respective rooms, since they were sold out for the day and had to prepare the rooms after cleaning and all. We tried to reach out to the Airlines staff but couldn't and had no option but to wait in the Hotel lobby. The Hotel guys weren't very willing to contact the airlines either. After a long wait of nearly two hours the buses finally arrived at 11 am and as we queued up to board there was an announcement that we were going to another Hotel- Thistle, if I remember the name correctly, since the aircraft wasn't ready to fly!

Fifteen minutes' drive and we reached our new destination and checked in. We were told at the reception that the buffet lunch was ready at the ground floor restaurant. The spread although was limited to typically Indian food but was sumptuous and delicious, indeed. Since we didn't have much to do, the four of us settled down at a cozy corner table and enjoyed the food. Meanwhile, the Airlines Manager was moving round, visiting each table meeting the guests who had stayed overnight. Although the hospitality was quite decent, the fact remains that we were rather cheesed off because of the snag first followed by an overnight stay and then the change of hotels leading to a feeling of shear frustration and uncertainty.

He came to our table as well and asked about our wellbeing. We thanked him and told him that we understood that things were beyond his control and acknowledged the courtesy that was extended on his part. He asked us what else he could do to make our transit more comfortable. On this I said, *"Yes, of course you can do a little more to make our stay memorable. Since yesterday, the departure of our flight back to New Delhi has been rescheduled twice, and even now there seems to be no certainty on how long it will take the plane to take off."* I continued, *"Mr. Manager, tomorrow being a Saturday, we don't mind staying back here over the weekend enjoying your hospitality if you allow complementary travel of our spouses from New Delhi to join us here by this evening's flight!"*

Well, the Manager didn't find it amusing at all. He immediately stood up and said that it was an unusual incident and happens only occasionally. Despite the challenges, he emphasized his commitment to managing the stranded passengers effectively. Apologizing sincerely, he guaranteed us that the flight would indeed depart later that evening. Despite the hiccups, we expressed our gratitude, recognizing his earnest efforts to ensure our comfort.

That evening, the flight finally took off at 5.30 pm from Heathrow and we landed at Delhi *'de-iced'*, safe and sound the next morning.

Incidentally, the Air France Flight 447, an Airbus A330, had crashed on June 1, 2009, in mid Atlantic after it was caught in an overnight thunderstorm several hours after leaving Rio-de-Janeiro for Paris. Ice crystals threw off the plane's airspeed sensors and its autopilot got disconnected leading to the fatal incident.

As they say, safety first is safety always. Prepare and prevent, don't repair and repent!

Section-II Corporate Dynamics

Naïve That I Was!

Let me take you back to the year 1980, a time when getting a decent job was akin to winning a battle despite having a stellar academic record. This was because of limited openings and cut-throat competition. It was under these challenging circumstances that I embarked on my journey towards a coveted position in ONGC, the National Oil Company of India.

As the announcement for executive positions in ONGC was made, I eagerly applied for the Geology and Palynology disciplines, the two fields in which I stood qualified based upon the laid down criteria. While Geology might be a familiar term to most, Palynology remained a hidden gem in the world of Geosciences. This intriguing discipline revolved around the study of pollen grains, especially those found in ancient geological rocks and deposits. Palynology, while relatively lesser known, plays a pivotal role in the quest for oil and gas reserves.

Having completed my Masters in Geology from Lucknow University in 1979, my heart was set on a career in Geology. Palynology and other allied fields were my second choice. To my surprise, I received interview calls for both positions, and the interviews were slated to take place at ONGC's prestigious Institute of Petroleum Exploration, nestled in the picturesque valley of Dehradun, a tranquil town cradled at the foothills of the majestic Himalayas.

Back in those days, Dehradun was popularly known as a *town of grey hair and green hedges*, a serene haven of peace and tranquility. Today it has evolved into the bustling capital of Uttarakhand, a vibrant but overcrowded metropolis, sadly bereft of its former charm. ONGC's Institute has also undergone a transformation, being renamed as the Keshav Dev Malviya Institute of Petroleum Exploration (KDMIPE) in honor of the visionary Pt. Keshav Dev Malviya, a former oil minister.

On May 05 1980, while waiting in the impressive conference hall of the Institute, the candidates were told by the HR guy that the interviews will be held in an alphabetical order and as always my name being from 'S' be it my name or my surname, my turn was towards the last. There are advantages and disadvantages of being the last or one of the last ones- advantage is obvious that you get to know the interview trend from the interviewed candidates and disadvantage being that your anxiety level keeps increasing as the time passes!

KDM Institute of Petroleum Exploration

As the day wore on, I couldn't help but notice a peculiar trend. Most candidates who had applied for the Palynology position with a master's degree in Geology were swiftly turned away by the interview board. On inquiring, a fellow candidate told me that a big and burly looking man with a tobacco pipe in hand- apparently, the Chairman of Board asked him whether he had applied for Geologist's post and on saying yes, he asked him to go back and prepare for that interview since the vacancies for geology were many. (*Much later after joining ONGC, I came to know that the big-burly man was none other than the legendary petroleum geologist Mr. SN Talukdar*).

In alphabetical order, towards the end of the day when eventually my turn came, I too was told to go back by Mr. Talukdar. Not wanting to lose a job opportunity in those difficult days, I sought his permission to make a submission. I said that Palynology was an upcoming tool in oil exploration and being my favourite subject, I may be given a chance to be interviewed. He shot back in his gentle but firm voice "if you have to choose between the two which one will you opt for, man". I somehow gathered the courage to tell him that I would prefer to be a Palynologist rather than a Geologist in the Company. For a moment, he fixed his gaze upon me, then gestured for me to be seated. He beckoned Dr. Venkatchala, the subject matter expert, to commence the interview. My interview lasted for nearly 20 minutes and to me, my performance appeared to be quite satisfying. I came out jubilant, as this was a victorious moment for me, not just because of the prospect of employment but because I had successfully made my case.

After a few days, on the 12th of May, when I appeared for my interview for the Geologist's post, to my utter surprise the Chairman of the Board was again none other than Mr. Talukdar. A quick thought flashed across my mind- if he recognized me and remembered my answer to him during my last interview, I am doomed. A little shaky, I was engrossed in these thoughts, when he greeted me- "Yes Sharma, you have come again. You are a Geology graduate, right! Now tell me which of the two disciplines you feel is better as a career for you in ONGC". Being a fresher and naïve in these matters, I had never expected that the Chairman for the two interview boards would be the same and even if the Chairman was same, he would remember me after seven days when he was conducting so many interviews daily. (*Later I came to know that Mr. Talukdar had an exceptionally sharp memory*).

 I was caught in my own trap! Sheepishly, I replied- "Sir, both are equally good". Magnanimous as he was, he laughed heartily and said, 'Clever man, don't give a diplomatic answer' and told Dr. Biswas, another excellent geoscientist, and the Board Member to carry on with my interview as he had seen my performance in the last interview and proceeded to his Desk to attend to some urgent work.

In August 1980, I got the appointment intimation through a telegram for Geologist in Class-I grade but was kept at waitlist-1 in the other interview. I joined my assignment in early September 1980 and never left the Company till superannuation in 2018.

Indeed, Talukdar Sir had an elephantine memory and a heart of gold that I witnessed again and again in my early days in ONGC till he was there.

My Early 'Gurus'

Back in September 1980, I got onboard a fascinating journey with ONGC as a graduate trainee. The story begins in Dehradun, where I found myself at the very Institute in which my induction interview took place. It was here that I became part of an interesting project sponsored by the National Council of Science and Technology (NCST). The project's mission was to unveil the secrets hidden beneath the Indian west coast using specialized techniques. It aimed to decipher the enigmatic paleo-depositional history and the hidden world of subsurface geology, all by employing the intriguing principle of *'Present is key to the Past.'* This concept suggests that by studying the sediment deposition processes occurring today in the oceans, we can gain insights into what transpired here millions of years ago. Isn't it a captivating thought? Unraveling the past by observing the present, all in the pursuit of discovering more oil and gas.

I was new to the set up and trying to give my best in a team of four geoscientists with a supervisor who happened to be an exceptional geoscientist, Mr. PC Dhar- may his soul rest in eternal peace, he passed away a few months ago. Though he explained to me in detail the nuances of the project but being a very busy man, I didn't want to trouble him for small things. I took it upon myself to address issues independently or collaborate with the section in-charges of the laboratories I worked in. This was my way of finding my footing in this exciting new environment.

One such interaction with a Section In-charge turned out to be a great learning experience for me. Given that the project involved studying the thin sections of the sea-bottom sediments, I was spending most of my time on Microscopes identifying the mineral and fossil constituents of the sediments. During my Master's, I had used microscopes in the University but the ones in the Institute were very advanced German *Leitz microscopes* with powerful magnifications and fitted with thin section photography camera instruments. I managed to photograph the thin sections but to understand how to calculate the magnification of the photographs shot under these microscopes, I decided to take guidance from Dr. MLS, the In-charge of Petrography Laboratory. Incidentally, the thin section study under the microscope is known as *Petrography*.

Dr. MLS had a very charismatic personality and would always seem extremely busy moving at his signature pace with his head slightly tilted towards the right, through the long corridors of the Institute. Some of the freshers felt that he resembles Joy Mukherji- yes, indeed he had an uncanny resemblance with the popular Bollywood star! Dr. MLS welcomed me into his room, patiently heard my dilemma about calculation of the magnification with his eyes closed, asked me to sit down and started looking out of the window.

A while later, he turned his head towards me with a jerk and said in a soft whisper-like tone, 'Mr. Sharma there are two ways to address your problem- the easier one is that I sit with you in the Petrography Lab, spend an hour from my time and explain to you what it is all about.' He paused for a moment looking directly into my eyes and then continued 'the other way – a rather difficult one -is that we have a big Library here on the first floor, you may go there, spend time, and look for manuals and books, you will find about 4-5 books on the subject, go through them. Come back to the Lab, try on your own and if you still find it perplexing, I am always there for you!' he told me with a broad smile.

I stood up and thanked him but before I could leave, he asked me, 'Mr. Sharma you didn't tell me which approach you would prefer'. I strode towards the library and once there, I found that the library was a vast treasure trove of books, scientific journals, monographs and ONGC's unpublished reports- a treasure to cherish, which I always visited whenever I happened to be in the Institute, even after I was posted out of Dehradun. Those were the days when internet was unheard of, and we depended on Libraries for any referral work- the good old days indeed- an era to look back on with fondness!

This was my first Guru in my formative years who knowingly or unknowingly taught me to be self-reliant and to avoid shortcuts. But I also made it a point to help my colleagues, if I could in any way throughout my entire career. He did meet me pacing up the corridor a couple of days later and asked, 'Mr. Sharma, could you find a solution to your problem or do I help you out.' I thanked him once again. He had given me a solution which helped me all through my career, even today.

My next Guru. The very first month-end was approaching, and a senior colleague, sensing my newness to the organization advised me to contact the enigmatic finance guy responsible for the intricate dance of paperwork required to secure my first salary. He further told me that next month onwards the process would be streamlined, regularized and the salary will go to the Bank directly. I went looking for the concerned junior executive and located him sitting on his rather diminutive wooden desk in the middle of a big Hall that housed the finance and accounts wing of the Institute. There were numerous other junior executives sitting in this Hall.

I approached his desk and greeted him but he seemed more interested in his numerical labyrinth. A minute passed and I tried another greeting. This time, without lifting his head, he gestured for me to sit on a humble wooden stool kept next to his chair. Eventually, he peered over his spectacles, which were perched at the tip of his nose and asked, "New joining?" I nodded and he produced a pink-colored form with two additional sheets and handed them over. "Fill these out in triplicate and bring them back tomorrow," he said. And so, I left with my mission in hand.

I diligently filled out the forms and returned to submit them the next day. This time also he gave me the same welcome as was on my first visit to him. He didn't care to look up and I kept standing for a while in front of him. When I greeted him again, he said that he was very busy checking the payrolls and asked me to leave the form in an olive green coloured metal tray kept on his desk and come again the next day. Though a little put off, I kept my cool out of the enthusiasm of getting my first salary. Also, I was very new in the organization. The next day was the last Friday of the month and happened to be the salary day, as well. Being a little busy in the forenoon, I reached his desk at around 2.30 pm and again found him engrossed or pretending to be engrossed in some papers. But to my surprise, this time he at once offered me the *guest-stool* to sit on.

It seemed that he had morphed into a friendlier version of himself! I sat on the stool and kept on sitting there for nearly 10 minutes when he suddenly opened the uppermost wooden drawer to his right with an abrupt jerk and pulled out my salary voucher duly approved and signed all over by various authorities. He handed it to me and pointed to the wall clock, which ominously signalled 2:45 pm. "Rush to the Cash counter, they close at 3 pm sharp," he commanded. "Today is the salary day, so expect a rush." My hopes of getting my first salary were fading fast. I grabbed the voucher and sprinted to the cash counter. I barely made it, being the last one in the room before it was locked from inside.

After I collected my salary, fuming with frustration, I stormed back to this finance gentleman's desk. I confronted him, demanding an explanation for making me chase my salary for three days. Smiling mischievously, he stood up and congratulated me on my first salary. He then asked me to sit and offered me a cup of tea – incidentally the tea vendor was there at that point in the time, it being 3 pm. Now sitting relaxed he explained, 'I was expecting that you would come back to confront me but believe me what I did was for your good in the longer run'. He further told me of his good and bad experiences of dealing with the new executives who came from different walks of life and different backgrounds, some with sky-high expectations, often being unaccommodating and averse to the Institute-culture.

His philosophy, he explained, was to make them realize that here, everyone is on an equal footing and one need not take any department for granted, so he preferred to have a snappy approach in the very beginning. He chuckled and said, 'I knew your anxiousness about your first salary and when you didn't come in the forenoon, I had requested the cash counter guys in advance not to close the counter before paying you your salary today!

Perplexed, I thanked him for the tea and left his desk pondering the wisdom hidden behind his initially gruff conduct. As the years rolled by, I realized that the lesson I learned from this peculiar gentleman had served me well in nurturing excellent relationships with various departments throughout my 38-year career in the company.

Who would have thought that my first salary would come with such a quirky twist!

Seas of Turmoil

Dehradun, a place of grace and charm, truly comes to life in the seasons of Spring and Autumn when the weather is at its best, neither hot nor too cold. During the Spring, there's a symphony of all round fragrance of *Madhumalti* (Rangoon Creeper), *Raat ki Rani* (Night Jasmine) and many more flowers blooming in unison. The majestic, tall Silver Oak trees and the beautiful Gulmohar (*Royal poinciana*) with orange flowers flourishing in the Valley creating a magnificent spectacle. Autumn, often linked with melancholy in the western world, holds a different meaning in Dehradun. It's a welcome respite from the hot summer, bringing a refreshing coolness to the air as September arrives.

It was one such pleasant morning during end of October 1981 when on reaching my Institute I was greeted by the postman with a telegram which had its origin in Goa. It wasn't a surprise to me because I knew that my Project Leader Mr. Dhar was on a visit to the National Institute of Oceanography (NIO) in Goa. Our project on ocean bottom study was in collaboration with NIO, Goa and envisaged a Cruise in the Arabian Sea to collect the ocean bottom sediment samples and other data for analysis, interpretation and recommendations towards the defined objective of the project.

The telegram was from Mr. Dhar intimating the Cruise date which was scheduled within the next four days. In those days, internet and mobile phones were unheard of and the fastest mode of communication was through telegrams and subscriber trunk dialing (STD). In another minute, my desk phone rang up with a long continuous tone- a lightening call. It was Mr. Dhar who told me to put up an official note to the Admin wing about the two of us- I and a colleague to proceed immediately to Goa to board the Cruise. He also told me to come prepared to be on the ship for two weeks.

We weren't entitled to travel by air then, but the urgency of the work gave us an opportunity to travel by air from Delhi to Goa via Mumbai (then Bombay)- the excitement was at its peak- *the first air travel, a visit to Goa and a two weeklong Cruise*- everything was so exhilarating and tempting! We packed our bags, collected the tickets from the Admin Wing of the Institute and the next day boarded the night bus to Delhi. The following morning, we reached Mumbai by Indian Airlines and straightway went to board the connecting flight to Goa at the Mumbai Airport. Little did we realize that in the excitement of this dream trip, we had forgotten to notice that the Mumbai-Goa flight tickets were waitlisted. Our enthusiasm was met with a reality check when we were denied entry onto the flight despite our insistence initially, then followed by pleas, since it was full. We were directed to the Airport Duty Manager.

In those days, the only airline operating on the domestic routes was the national carrier – Indian Airlines and there were very few flights- most departures took place by the forenoon. That day also, the departure terminal at Mumbai airport wore a deserted look by the afternoon, and we didn't find it very difficult to locate the Duty Manager- a seemingly middle-aged, bespectacled lady, perched on a slight highchair behind the counter. Desperate, I explained to her the entire emergency like situation for us because the Cruise was to start in another three days.

She listened to our predicament with her full attention but expressed her inability to help us since there was only one daily flight to Goa and it was full, and about to take off. I told her about the fact that every single day of delay will cost nearly twenty-six thousand rupees to our Institute towards the waiting charges of the cruise ship but she expressed her helplessness. She told us to come an hour earlier the next day and promised that she would push our case. She assured us of seats if there was no unplanned VIP movement.

My colleague who was till now silently listening to the conversation suddenly blurted out, 'Don't you understand Miss, we are travelling by Air! Such is the urgency of our mission. You people should be accommodative in such critical circumstances.' Probably, she was not ready for this. Taken aback, she frowned, stared at him with her big eyes looking even bigger behind the thick lenses she wore and shot back, 'Gentleman, this is an airport, not a railway station. Whosoever comes here is travelling by air and not by train or bus!' And she got up with a whimper and left the Counter in a huff!

Nevertheless, we did get our seats the next day, thanks to the lady, and reached Goa in time to board the cruise with a day to spare for preparations and discussions on the schedule with the Project Leader and the NIO team that was to accompany us. The next day early in the morning, we boarded the ship named 'RV Gaveshani'. RV stands for Research Vessel. Gaveshani was a huge barge, bought by NIO a few years ago and converted into a scientific vessel with provision for sea bottom sample collection and certain other data collection facilities.

The plan was to first travel north directly to Porbandar, off Gujarat coast, in two and a half days' time- anchor the ship off Porbandar, refuel, collect rations, and then start sample and data collection activity round-the-clock, in 8 east to west traverses (trips) from Porbandar offshore down to Goa during the next ten days. The ship was to halt every two and a half hours for one hour for this purpose when we would come on to the deck, lower the winch, collect samples and other data, label and mark systematically and go back to our cabins, as the ship would move on for the next station. These 8 traverses were almost equidistant all along the Indian coastline aligned perpendicular to it and the last traverse was to end a little north of Goa.

From ONGC and NIO, we were about 10 geoscientists and of course the crew, kitchen and other staff. It was an excellent team, we had developed a good understanding among us the geoscientists on the very first day and were having discussions on a wide variety of topics, playing indoor games like carrom, scrabble or just reading a book or a magazine. We had good cabins to us on twin-sharing basis complete with two berths and two cupboards, two study tables with lamps and a small wash basin.

It was a clear sky when we left Goa, but little did we know what was in store for us in just the next 16 hours. From midnight itself, we had started experiencing rolling and pitching of the ship, which we thought was routine since for few of us it was a maiden experience in the sea. We were up early in the morning to realize that the sea was quite rough by this time. Using the washroom and bathing cabin was a challenge that required a real balancing act because of the turbulence. We somehow managed to get ready and went up to the dining hall located on level-one on the deck for breakfast at around 7 am.

It was then that we saw the overcast sky and the choppy sea with fast winds blowing. The ship seemed unstable struggling in the gusty winds. We had just settled for breakfast when there was an announcement by the ship's Captain- Commander Mathews (*probably that was his name, if I remember it correctly*) on the speakerphone warning all of us about the approaching cyclone! He commanded all of us to return to our cabins within 15 minutes and stay put till the weather cleared, maybe in a few hours or a couple of days even. He also cautioned us to be extremely careful while walking through the passages of the ship and not to remain empty stomach to avoid puking, if the turbulence worsens.

The announcement was barely over when suddenly, the gentleman sitting opposite me in the dining hall shouted, 'See the wave, See the wave.' We all looked outside of the porthole and it was a giant wall of seawater about 10 feet high approaching the ship at a lightning speed. And before we could react, the ship tilted sharply towards one side with all the breakfast, cutlery and crockery flying off our tables. We could barely stay put by holding tight on to the 4-seater dining tables which were fixed to the floor. And as the giant wave went below the ship, we all nearly tossed up on our seats and then the ship got tilted to the other side, with everything coming back rolling on to this side.

As this continued with increasing intensity and frequency, we decided to grab a couple of apples and bananas which were now scattered all over the floor and rushed back to our cabins balancing ourselves in the heavy rolling and pitching. Since RV Gaveshani was earlier a huge barge, it was flat-bottomed unlike the regular ships which have a 'keel' at the bottom to provide stability while sailing and more so in bad weather. In a flat-bottomed vessel the effect of rolling and pitching increased manifolds.

I had earlier read that extreme weather conditions induce severe sea sickness frequently causing giddiness, killing the appetite and leads to puking. Worse is when prolonged empty stomach conditions in a turbulent sea causes damage to the stomach lining resulting in throwing up blood even- a serious condition indeed. Hence, it's recommended that no matter how sick you are, you should not totally stop eating or drinking. The idea is to eat, drink and then throw up but don't stop eating or drinking!

But as luck would have it, by the evening that day, one of the two generators on the ship conked off. The captain and the chief engineer diverted the available electricity to keep the engines running and radars functional. As a result, the electricity supply to the kitchen where the deep freezers were kept was cut. Only the corridors and the medical room had moderate intensity lighting, even our cabins had very dim lights. That ominous night none of us could sleep- the roar of the waves, severe rolling & pitching and the worsening weather was frightening. By the morning, except for a handful inmates of the ship, everyone was sea-sick throwing up intermittently, often blood. The lemons and oranges were all consumed, all other food material had perished since there wasn't any electricity for over 15 hours.

Under these circumstances, some advice from an elderly crew member came as Godsend. He was in our cabin with a message from the Project Leader.

I noticed that he had a bottle of the local Goan brew- Cashew Feni in his hand and was intermittently taking small sips from it. He told us that there's nothing to eat or drink on the ship except for some dry rations like nuts, candies and salty snacks which can be had only in limited amounts. Either you don't get up at all from your bunker bed or if you want to move for a while now and then, plain water wouldn't help much in alleviating the seasickness though lemonade or the alcohol in limited quantity would always help, he said with his long sailing experience. Hey presto! We just remembered that we were carrying with us a couple of whiskey bottles each. We jumped out of our beds and unpacked the bottles and kept a bottle each of *Peter Scot Whiskey* alongside our pillows. Then onwards, we would often sip the divine elixir hence escaped any kind of seasickness during this ordeal which lasted for nearly three days.

That day in the late afternoon, Captain Mathews and Mr. Dhar were on a round, meeting with everybody onboard- the staff, the crew, and the geoscientists to boost the dwindling morale. Surprisingly, they both looked or they pretended to look unperturbed and cool. The captain was a short, stout, cheerful man, he laughed and said it's just another cyclone and that he had steered this very vessel out of worse cyclonic situations in Bay of Bengal which is infamous for notoriety of the Sea. He also narrated his most harrowing experience once when Gaveshani got stuck in a twin cyclonic situation in the Bay of Bengal and he had a tough time salvaging the vessel. Mr. Dhar also seemed to be a tough guy as he had spent his younger days on fishing trawlers in east Bengal and had faced such situations before.

While we were listening to the stories about Gaveshani, a colleague suddenly demanded that the ship be taken back to the nearest shore to escape the wrath of the cyclone which seemed like increasing with every passing minute and looked like an unending ordeal. The captain very patiently explained to him that under such conditions taking any ship on the coast would be disastrous because the waves become very dangerous closer to the coast in low water depths.

An argument followed and the gentleman became hysterical, shouting that the crew and all onboard would be responsible if anything happened to him as he's the lone bread winner for his family – a wife, two small children and old parents. Mr. Dhar handled the situation very well and brought him under control as the guy eventually broke down crying on Mr. Dhar's shoulder. Mr. Dhar hugged him and reassured him that he was in safe hands and that he was not alone in this situation.

That day, we later came to know that the ship's radar and the engines had both malfunctioned late in the evening, and we were adrift in the Arabian Sea at the mercy of the winds and the sea waves. Since the sky was overcast, the age-old navigation methods of sailing weren't working as well. The captain was round-the-clock perched on the Bridge located on the upper deck steering the ship and Mr. Dhar keeping him company. The bridge being high is worst affected by rolling and pitching but the secret of the two gentlemen staying up and about was again the local brew Cashew Fenni- in regular but small sips!

Around midnight, I suddenly got up hearing the commotion in the corridor. I jumped out of my berth and came out to see a couple of seamen rushing down the corridor towards the stairs for engine room. On asking they hurriedly told me that there's a leak in the engine room and the sea water had started seeping in- a dangerous situation indeed, especially when everything was failing- the generators, the engine, the radar and now this. It was a frightening situation indeed. I followed them and on reaching the engine room found that the water had started accumulating inside, though in small quantities. The situation could turn alarming if remedial measures weren't immediately taken. The captain and the chief engineer were already there struggling to repair the engines and the generator.

Hats off to the ship's engineering team- in half an hour's time, the generator started working and the crew could also contain the leakage by patching up the seepage spot. Another hour's struggle under the dim lights and the engineers could successfully restart the engines. They had all worked non-stop for the last 12 hours to bring back the ship under control. The captain now rushed to the bridge to reset and reactivate the radars and check the ship's location. Whoop! We were drifting in international waters much towards our neighbour! But the good news was that the cyclone had weakened by then as it had moved across the Saurashtra coast into the land. The captain started steering the vessel back on track to Porbandar at full throttle.

By the time it was morning, the cyclonic winds had vanished, and we got up to a clear blue sky. Most of the sick were also up and about and we were on the deck enjoying the clear weather after two nightmarish nights and three days. But it came as a shock to us when we noticed a few wooden and metal debris afloat on the seawater along with a big green suitcase. The captain who was catching up on sleep in his cabin, after this ordeal, later told us that there was a Mayday call during the midnight from a nearby ship which had run low on fuel. The mid-sea fuel transfer could not have happened due to the rough sea conditions. Could it be that ill-fated ship or something else, we were wondering.

For us, the relief was palpable as we found ourselves back on course to Porbandar, navigating the calm seas at full throttle. With the storm behind us, a sense of euphoria washed over the ship's occupants, as we enjoyed the cool morning breeze. Though nothing was left on the ship to eat or drink except for limited dry rations and drinking water. To our relief, the chef took matters into his hands and his team could be seen fishing on the deck as we made our way to Porbandar, where we would soon replenish our stocks.

While the ordeal had ended, our journey had just begun - a calamitous yet unforgettable cruise in the seas of turmoil, forever etched in our memories!

The Indian Express, dated November 02, 1981 reported, *"Over 1,400 fishermen from Gujarat and Maharashtra have been reported missing in the Arabian Sea, a fishermen's colony of over 100 huts in Rajapur port town has been swept away and four persons were feared drowned as the Saurashtra coast reeled under a severe cyclonic storm. At least two cargo vessels sank, several boats capsized and the communication network was crippled. The storm was expected to cross the coast between Veraval and Porbandar by midnight on November 1 and re-emerge as a cyclone in the Gulf of Kutch on November 2. Earlier in the day, a bauxite-laden ship sank near Veraval."*

During this ominous maritime occurrence rated under Category 1- very severe cyclonic storm, a wind velocity reaching 120 km/h was documented by the Indian Meteorological Department.

We were thankful to the Almighty that we had survived- was it our stars or the extolled RV Gaveshani that had a history of survival under the worst of sea storms. Who knows!

Himalayan Challenge

Dehradun, as I mentioned earlier, used to be a sleepy town in the early eighties and known as a *city of grey hair and green hedges-* with most of the population comprising superannuated personnel from the defence, government and educational institutions. Dehradun has been home to unique institutions like Forest Research Institute, Indian Military Academy, Survey of India, Naval Hydrology Institute, Indian Institute of Petroleum and of course the ONGC. These institutions had chosen this idyllic setting, with its serene surroundings and a charming British legacy. Other than a handful of personnel working in these institutions and the local merchants, the city has several famous schools which provide the right environment for studies and sports in a tranquil backdrop.

The town falls in Doon Valley which used to be thickly forested, mostly with tall and elegant Sal trees (*Shorea robusta*) all around, intersected by numerous streams and rivers most of which were seasonal in nature. However, over time, the forest cover has dwindled drastically, and the rivers are transformed into garbage-filled drains due to what many termed "development," especially after Uttarakhand was granted statehood in the early 21st century. Echoing these sentiments, Ruskin

Bond, the renowned author and laureate aptly stated, "*I may have stopped loving Dehradun now, but I can't stop loving the days, I loved Dehradun*."

It was a 6-day week work culture then, the second Saturdays being closed holidays. We used to frequently venture out on the weekends- a small group of like-minded friends, a couple of them married as well! Places like Asarodi & Mohand to the south, Kansaro, Phandowala & Lacchiwala towards east, Mussoorie, Kempty Falls & Dhanaulti to the north and Rampur Mandi & Paonta to the west were a few favourites. In those days, it was easy to get the Forest Division guest houses booked at a nominal cost and we would pack our bags with a few beer bottles, green peas, uncooked fish and loads of snacks and cold drinks to settle down in one of these places mostly to spend the day. After a week's hard work, these getaways were refreshing and full of fun.

On one such trip to Phandowala, now under Rajaji National Park, the idea of longer outings and challenging treks or even mountaineering evolved. The imaginations started taking flight- why not form an Association of like-minded enthusiasts in ONGC. During this time, Col SP Wahi was the Chairman of ONGC who encouraged the sporting and extra-curricular activities among the executives and staff.

This idea of trekking and mountaineering through an Association, somehow reached the then Member (Personnel) of ONGC through informal discussions with some colleagues. He agreed to the idea on the condition that the boys should first prove themselves, then only the ONGC Board would recognize the "ONGC Himalayan Association" formally. Mr. Pande, a geologist of Antarctica Expedition fame (*later retired from ONGC as Director Exploration*) was summoned and conveyed the conditional acceptance of the Member Personnel.

This momentous day filled us with joy. We quickly formed an informal body, with AP Ghosh as President, Indira Kohli as VP, DK Pande, Secretary, Sacchanand as Treasurer, Rakesh Rastogi and I as Joint Secretaries. Alongside a membership campaign, we started scouting for a reasonably challenging trek in the Himalayas. After multiple rounds of discussions with Garhwal Vikas Mandal Nigam (GMVN) offices in Dehradun and Rishikesh, we settled on a trek to the "Yamunotri Pass". Little did we know that what we presumed to be a moderately challenging trek would prove to be a genuinely formidable endeavour. Despite initial apprehensions, we rallied around twenty members of which thirteen brave souls agreed to undertake the adventure, ascending to approximately 14,500 feet. As told to us, the trek encompassed nearly seven days of traversing the breathtaking landscapes of the Garhwal Himalayas.

Next on the list was to arrange the trekking/ mountaineering gear for all of us like ice-axes, trekking boots, rucksacks, sleeping bags, ropes & knuckles, snow goggles, trek-suits, jackets, head gear with torchlights, water bottles, and tents. Dry rations including Theraptin biscuits, essential medicines, sunscreen lotions and more. The inventory kept growing by day since all were new to this adventure. The local market and GMVN offices in Dehradun and Rishikesh were scoured for equipment, but the supply was woefully inadequate. We could barely manage to hire just 6 ice axes, ruck sacks for all, 6 trekking boots (*most of us used Bata Hunters which were very popular in those days*), some ropes & knuckles, 6 or 7 snow goggles, few head gear with torches. The trekking and mountaineering equipment was very scarce in the local market. So, we had to depend on our personal belongings for many of the essential items also. To meet all these expenses including transport to the starting point, porter expenses and stay, we collected Rs 200 each and requested a grant of Rs. 2500 from our management. We were granted Rs. 2000. The scrutiny was so stringent that looking at 'Avomin' on the OTC medicine list, there was a comment- 'why Avomin? Are any pregnant ladies also on the trek'. Though it was in a lighter vein but such was the scrutiny!

Finally, a team of 13 ONGCians with DK Pande, as the Team Leader were ready for the assault- RK Sharma, VK Gupta, BG Samanta, Saumitra Gupta, BK Dey, T.Sanyal, DN Singh, Subimal Kar, S. Chakravarty, P. Unnikrishnan, Sacchanand, Rakesh Rastogi and yours truely. I was the official photographer on the trek, carrying two cameras- a fixed lens Pentax for colour photography and an SLR Zenit for B&W captures. All packed up and in high spirits, we started our journey from Dehradun by bus on June 06, 1982 early in the morning.

As we stopped at Vikasnagar for breakfast, Dr. VK Gupta- a psychologist by profession distributed a set of forms to all of us with multiple questions about our perception towards many things – a psychology test which was to be repeated with similar set of questions at the Summit and once again on our return. He intended to do an analysis of how a person's perception changes towards various things in life under different mental states before, during and after the trek.

The trek started on June 07, 1982 and we reached a place popularly called Talao (? Saptrishi Kund), at the base of Bandarpunch Glacier on June 11, 1982. The entire five days of trek was very picturesque through the dense jungles, meadows and valleys but sometimes treacherous as well, and certainly quite exhausting. The villages on the way were clean and beautiful. We generally spent the nights in or around them and enjoyed the local delicious food. We were traversing nearly 10-11 kms everyday mostly uphill!

On the way, we occasionally met nomads- *the van gujjars* with their cattle grazing in the lush green meadows near their temporary settlements. They were always ready to pose for a photograph or two, especially the children and the youngsters. I asked one of them why were they so keen on photographs when they knew that they would not be able to get to see any of those. This little boy very innocently replied in the local dialect, "It's for you, so that you remember meeting me here. Today we are here, tomorrow we will be gone. But one day, if Almighty permits I will meet you again. Please keep my photo with you." It was indeed a very touchy statement from this innocent kid- I have these photographs with me even today properly arranged in an Album.

Nestled in a quaint Dharamshala in Talao, we gazed out at the mesmerizing scene- a serene pond, surrounded by pristine, snow-covered mountains. As we settled in, our eyes couldn't help but wander to the colorful tents not very far. The stage was set for an unexpected encounter!

The exotic Van Gujjars posing for a photograph

Around 4 pm, a group of 8-10 young women arrived from the northern side of the pond. They swiftly disappeared into the awaiting tents. These were no ordinary travellers, they were a team of intrepid lady mountaineers, on a mission to trek across the formidable Bandarpunch Glacier. Their expedition was under the expert guidance of Brigadier B.S. Sandhu, the Principal of the National Institute of Mountaineering (NIM) – an Arjuna Awardee in the world of mountaineering.

This was a golden opportunity for us to meet him and take tips for our Yamunotri Pass assault that was planned in the next two days. Our team leader went to meet him and explained to him the entire trip, its objective, the team that was untrained, the equipment and so on.

Tents pitched near Talao

The veteran was initially pleasantly surprised but shocked later, when he heard that we were inadequately equipped and we weren't trained even in the basics of mountaineering.

He told categorically that the trek we had unknowingly selected was a treacherous one and the team should acclimatize for at least two days before the final assault. What he was saying was correct but we didn't had any rations or resources left to support the two days of acclimatization. He shared that the Bandarpunch glacier was a less complicated trek compared to the Yamunotri Pass but still he was going for three days of acclimatization. A while later, he visited and met each one of us and cheered all of us in his typical armed forces manner. He gave some useful tips on snow trekking, the correct way of using ice axes, overnight tent pitching and most importantly the caution required while descending snow-clad slopes. He wished us luck and left promising to reunite in Dehradun upon our return. We got up early in the morning the next day on June 12 and embarked on the trek which was not only long but mostly on the snow.

A day before the snow trek

It was an awesome trek lasting nearly eight hrs with snow all around. Since the sky was overcast, there wasn't any sunlight making it dangerous to maneuver the snow at places which were icy and slippery. In such situations, proper training in using ropes and ice axes comes in handy. Our local guide helped us identify a safe spot to pitch the tents. It was too cold around 4 pm with snow all around and we yearned for a cup of hot tea.

Setting up a portable gas cylinder with a saucepan filled with snow seemed like the solution. But the bitter cold prolonged the process, taking nearly 15 minutes for the snow to melt into water. Then, disaster struck- the mini gas cylinder tipped over and sank into the snow. Frustrated and impatient, none of us had the fortitude to go through the tea-making ordeal again. Our super early dinner that night consisted of just a few Theraptin biscuits each. Cold and weary, we retreated into our two-seater tents, bracing ourselves for the next day, which was anticipated to be the longest and toughest of all.

On June 13, we rose at 3 am, hastily performed our morning routines, and savoured a cup of lukewarm tea. We set off for the final stretch of our journey. After trekking for a while, we noticed that it was a clear blue sky with a bright sun shining above us at around 0530 am. In another two hours, we came across a 100m high wall of snow which had to be negotiated to reach the Yamnotri Pass. We paused for a while to discuss the approach strategy. We opted for a lengthy, zigzagging approach to conquer this steep escarpment.

As we started to move, we encountered an unexpected obstacle. One of our team members abruptly stopped, sat down, and refused to move ahead. No amount of persuasion would convince him to proceed, and he insisted on turning back, even if alone. Our guide grew increasingly concerned, sensing the potential danger of an avalanche triggered by a massive block of ice jutting out over our path, given the sunny day. We decided to leave him to himself for some time with a couple of us around him and the rest of the group started the ascent. He kept sitting there on his haunches for a while and then suddenly got up singing the song- *'we shall overcome one day'* with his right hand triumphantly raised. We gave a big sigh of relief!

As we all climbed up to a place where the Pass was visible, we heard a loud thud followed by a roar and a cloud of snow could be seen in the sky behind us- the avalanche had struck. Miraculously, we had timed our climb just right, thanks to the divine blessings!

The day of Assault

We reached the Pass at around 1 pm that day on June 13, hoisted the ONGC Himalayan Association flag and celebrated with Theraptin biscuits! The atmosphere was full of joy with a fulfilling feeling of achievement – *we had done it!* We could see the

Yamunotri Peak nearby and the view from the top was spectacular.

I did my level best to capture the landscape and the jubilant team alike.

The final ascent

Against the popular notion of 13 as an unlucky number, our team of 13 achieved the extraordinary feat of scaling the Pass on June the 13th against all odds, affirming that the number 13 brought us remarkable fortune.

Those were the days when digital photography hadn't arrived, so one had to be very judicious while clicking pictures from the film rolls. While everyone was enjoying the stunning view all-round, Dr. Gupta insisted on filling up the psych-test forms- part II. We did that as the guide reminded us of the long and arduous way ahead and asked us to hurry up.

Thus began the descent, commencing with a 150-metre descent, interrupted by a large rock jutting out halfway down the slope.

We left the Pass at around 2.30 pm that day. Luckily for us, because of a clear day the upper layer of snow had softened up and all of us could

Conquering the Yamunotri Pass: A Triumph of Perseverance!

glide down in a sitting position with our rucksacks on our lap, controlling the speed by spreading our legs and putting our boots deep in the soft snow. At this point, a rather funny incident occurred. As nearly half the team had already reached the base of the slope, Gupta's bag, being carried by a porter, was flung into the air when the porter attempted to navigate the protruding rock. Tragically, the bag opened, and the psych-test sheets scattered into the sky. Poor Dr. Gupta found himself frantically chasing these precious sheets, which would serve as the foundation for his analysis of human psychology under various conditions, from anxiety to the joy of success and the fulfillment of this unique expedition. We did our best to assist him, but the soft snow impeded our progress, and time was of the essence. By this point, it was already 4:30 pm, and the darkness loomed. We trekked downhill along a steep escarpment for long in ankle-deep snow. It was a tough trek and had become tougher because of softened up snow.

But then, it was a blessing in disguise for us since we neither had adequate equipment nor were we trained to use it. We had wrapped pieces of

The Challenging Descent: Navigating the precarious path

polythene over our socks to avoid getting them wet

and cold in the melting snow. The trek under the setting sun and then bright moonlit night presented a breathtaking view of the snow-clad rock face with a silvery sheen.

It was 7.30 pm in the evening when we reached a snow-free area. We were dead tired by this time, trekking in snow since early morning with our feet almost frozen. After another 2 hours of steep climb down, we reached a spot known as 'Hariyali Thatch' and pitched the tents, removed the shoes and socks, warmed up our feet around a small bonfire for a while and straightaway hit our sleeping bags in the tents. Next morning, we trekked down to the famous Yamunotri Temple. Almost all of us took a plunge into the hot water pond in the premises and enjoyed the refreshing hot water bath. We stayed overnight and reached Dehradun via Janaki Chatti on June 15.

On returning to Dehradun, we were welcomed as heroes. As the month drew to a close, we had the honour of delivering a comprehensive presentation on our expedition at the prestigious AMN Ghosh Auditorium of the Institute. This remarkable event was graced by none other than the Chairman and the entire board of ONGC. Brigadier BS Sandhu was invited as a special Guest. He categorically said in his speech that when he had visited us in our camp at Talao, he had come mentally prepared to tell us to go back considering our preparedness but seeing our enthusiasm and high spirits he could not do so. Rather, he gave us important tips and suggestions for the assault. He also shared that a year back, his best instructor could not do this trek and had to abandon it halfway. He said, "It was the weather and the team's indomitable spirit that favoured the boys. Frankly speaking, I had fears in my heart that how many of them would I see ever again. But they were determined, they did it and a big cheer to all of them."

The function itself unfolded over two exhilarating hours, marking a pivotal moment in our journey. In July 1983, ONGC Himalayan Association (ONGCHA) received its well-deserved formal recognition, and from that point forward, there was no looking back. ONGCHA went on to achieve one milestone after another, culminating in the ultimate triumph in 2017- the conquest of Everest.

It's a remarkable journey that began with a casual discussion during our Phandowala sojourn and it's a testament to the incredible power of dreams and determination.

Isn't it simply amazing?

Pataal Ganga- the Hidden Oasis

On an unusually laid-back Monday morning, I found myself engrossed in the routine daily tasks when an unexpected summons from the Chief, Mr. Tikku, disrupted the monotony. After a brief inquiry into the progress of my ongoing project, he dropped a bombshell—I was to report to the enigmatic Dr. Kayal (name changed), head of another department, for an urgent assignment. It so happened that the then Union Petroleum Minister was visiting our Institute the coming Friday and amongst the agenda he also wanted to give a statement on the freshwater potential of the Ganga River Basin which runs all along the terai region of Himalayan foothills in India, Nepal and Bangladesh. The minister represented a constituency in Garhwal region of the Uttar Pradesh and was also the Minister for Commerce hence the desire for such a statement in the public interest, I thought. Probably, he wanted to appraise the people of the state and his constituency of the groundwater potential and the fertile nature of their habitat.

Dr. Kayal tagged along a very able executive with me and gave us 72 hours' time to submit a short and crisp report on the subject matter supported by data, colourful graphs and cartoons. Mind you, it was 1986 when everything was done by hand with the help of draftsmen for final drawings and typing done on electronic typewriters. The challenge was formidable, considering our tight deadline and the fact that freshwater resources were not our usual turf at ONGC—we were, after all, oilmen! Contemplating the ethical implications of delving into another realm, I shared my concerns with Dr. Kayal. The seasoned professional assured us that the Minister merely sought a factual statement about groundwater resources, which is very normal and there shouldn't be an issue.

Without wasting any time, Mathur my associate for this project and I huddled in my room to plan our moves for the next 72 hours and started cracking immediately. We visited our library, fished out a few relevant articles and chalked out the outline of the Report. We skipped lunch that day, went to the Institute of Soil and Water Conservation located next to our Institute in Dehradun, met the Director, obtained his permission to consult their library, gathered whatever that we could and were back by 4 pm. The idea was to collect as much data as we could during office hours and capitalize on the evening hours for integration.

Mathur, as planned left for Lucknow that evening by train, to fetch more data from the offices of State

Groundwater Board and Geological Survey of India. The whole of next day, he spent shuttling among the relevant Lucknow offices moving in a cycle-rickshaw utilizing official channels as well as his contacts to access the data and information, making notes from the referred material, and taking photocopies, especially of the graphs, cartoons, and pictures. He returned the next morning by train. By this time, we were left with 48 hours to screen, sort and compile the large amount of data that we had collected and bring everything in the presentable format of a report. I had completed much of the groundwork the previous day. Since Mathur had already read most of the material that he had made notes from, it was not so difficult to complete the write up quickly followed by the selection of the supporting sketches, data graphs and figure tables. We took special care to provide a list of all the references that we had consulted in making this report.

Just to share, about 240 billion cubic metres (BCM) of groundwater is present in the Ganga River basin tqday, of which India has the highest potential (165 BCM), followed by Bangladesh (64 BCM) and Nepal (11 BCM). Nearly half of it has already been harnessed for irrigation, domestic, industrial and other purposes.

Our first draft was ready by 6 pm that day. After the completion, we both separately read the report during the late night and early morning the following day. As a rule, I have always been in the habit of leaving a completed assignment at least for a day or two and revisit the same with a fresh mind to see if any improvements can be made before submission. In the instant case, we didn't have even a day to spare so we left it overnight! Once satisfied with the quality and content, we passed on the text to the typist and the drawings to the attached draftsman the very next morning. In an effort to minimize errors, one of us hovered over the typist, while the other kept a watchful eye on the draftsman. By late evening, the report was complete in all respects, ready for submission to Dr. Kayal the following morning—right on the brink of the looming deadline. With minor edits, Dr. Kayal accepted the report and instructed his office to reproduce 3 copies of this report by that evening.

Next day, the Minister was set to grace our Institute at 10 am. Dr Kayal in his characteristic manner told me in the late evening that I need to accompany him to see the Chairman at 9 am in his office building the next day to appraise him of the report. The catch? The Chairman's schedule was so jam-packed that my grand report appraisal had to happen in the elevator, during the 30-second descent from his first-floor office to the ground floor! It was told to me that a copy of report is already with the Chairman.

With military precision, I found myself in the Chairman's office lounge at 5 minutes to 9 am, sipping coffee when suddenly, Dr. Kayal burst in, urgently summoning me. As the Chairman walked into the lift, he looked at me and said, "Hey, young man, come along." I seized the moment, enlightening him about the freshwater potential of the Ganga River Basin in that swift elevator ride. To my delight, he nodded in approval, uttering a crisp "good work done" and proceeded towards his waiting office car.

Later, I heard that the meeting went off well and the minister left the town by that afternoon.

The next day in the morning when I settled down with a cup of tea in my balcony, I was greeted by the shock of the century—local newspaper headlines screaming '*ONGC discovers Pataal Ganga – a huge freshwater underground reservoir.*' The article in its full glory had all the details of the '*discovery*'- about the resource potential, its geographic spread, the fertile soil, etc. etc. An unnecessary spectacle, I thought, from an over-enthusiastic media.

I met Dr. Kayal as soon as he arrived in the office that morning. He told me that he was expecting me and shared my concern. He said that it was an error, probably inadvertent on the part of the media and reassured me that our report had adequately covered the references in the text, as well as, in the bibliography and we never claimed that 'Pataal Ganga' was ONGC's discovery hence not a reason to worry- our conscience was as clear as crystal. I remember that the following week after 3-4 days there was a small rejoinder from the Geological Survey of India on page 6 or 7 that 'Pataal Ganga' was neither a new discovery nor made by ONGC. It was reported by the GSI decades ago!

Innocent misquoting or negligent misquoting—take your pick, but certainly not a case of deceptive misquoting, I mused. Quite the rollercoaster ride for a report on groundwater potential!

Whispers of Wisdom

Once I found myself entangled in a dance between Academics and Adventure during my early career days. Both are exhilarating and rather complementary to each other, I believe. As they say, *'All work and no play make Jack a dull boy,'* when you are too involved in your profession you need an occasional break to replenish and rejuvenate yourself. But at times the circumstances are such that one must choose between the two. I too was in a similar situation during early 1983 and believe me, it turned out to be a tough decision.

It so happened that the Indian Army decided to organize the 'Trans-Himalayan Car Rally,' a glorious 3500-Kms escapade from Khardung La Pass in J&K to another formidable Pass in Tawang District of northeastern India. A motorized odyssey through some of the world's highest roads, all to be conquered in about a month's time. The agenda was to study the ecology, geology, and the flora and fauna of the region! Heights reaching 17,852 ft, glaciers, mountain passes—full of enthusiasm and excitement. ONGC, being one of the sponsors, got the golden opportunity to send a team of three in a

Jonga- the legendary Indian Army vehicle by Nissan. Incidentally, the acronym Jonga was for '*Jabalpur Ordnance and Guncarriage Assembly*'. The management declared a team of three from ONGC Himalayan Association which included me to represent the Organisation. We were to attend the hill driving, breakdown and survival training course in Srinagar, J&K in the months of April-May to prepare ourselves for the ostensibly challenging and adventurous expedition.

The Rally was planned for August 1983 to be formally flagged off by Hon'ble Giani Zail Singh, the then President of India. As this adrenaline-pumping plan was unfolding, the Exploration Directorate of ONGC was busy circulating a Memorandum seeking candidature for a newly initiated M.Tech. (Petroleum Exploration) Course at Indian School of Mines, Dhanbad (now IIT, Dhanbad). Naturally, I had as much interest in this as a cat does in swimming lessons, knowing well that it would be nearly impossible to get selected for just eight vacancies from a huge crowd of geoscientists in ONGC. However, a friend of mine brought an application form for me also when he went to the HQs to collect one for himself. I didn't fill out the form till almost the last day when this dear friend of mine insisted that I must fill it in. I did it reluctantly and placed it under the official channel for submission on the very last day.

I had forgotten about it when one day in the month of March, 1983 out of the blue an office order graced my desk listing the selected eight. Ironically, it contained my name, but guess whose wasn't. Yes, my friend's name was missing! We were wondering what the selection criteria could have been. This friend of mine was of course sad but determined as he is even today, he knew that he still stood a chance since this scheme was for 3 consecutive years. He gracefully accepted the situation and moved on. Believe me, he did get selected the next year.

However, I was in a big dilemma as both the opportunities were kind of *a once in a lifetime chance*. I took the advice of my seniors who suggested not to miss the opportunity of taking up the professional course as an ONGC sponsored candidate. This was a course specially designed for the ONGC geoscientists and a lot of thought process had gone behind the curriculum of 'applied' nature. On the contrary, my adventure-loving buddies told me not to withdraw my name from the Rally since I would never get this chance again, M.Tech. can be done anytime during the career. I thought and thought, took my parents' advice also. Eventually, the academics prevailed over adventure!

It's true that I never got another chance to participate in a Rally of that size and scale but it is also true that M.Tech. in Petroleum Exploration was a turning point in my career. Unfortunately, very few Universities offered courses of Applied and Professional nature in those days and this professional course gave all the 8 sponsored ONGCians a totally different perspective of the petroleum industry and exploration evaluation techniques. So, no regrets!

There were 4 freshers also with us in this batch. The course had a very rigorous curriculum with two semesters of 7 papers each with 36 hours per week of classes! We came to know that ISM had initially suggested a 4-semester course but our Member Exploration asked them to condense it to two semesters only, as it would not be practical to depute so many executives for 4 semesters, year after year in consecutive three such courses. It was a double whammy for us- first the very tough curriculum, that too with four freshers with us and secondly, we the eight candidates were all corporate executives who could not have settled for low grades under any circumstances- had to keep the ONGC flag high!

We were back to school routine, discipline and the hostel life after basking in the glory of corporate life for a few years. The first semester was rather event-free- all of us made a mark in our grades and we had a good rapport with the strictest of the professors like the formidable Prof. AN Dutta, because of our sincere attitude towards the studies. Frankly, we didn't have much to do on the campus except for studying. Our most thrilling escapade? The daily pilgrimage to Ramdhani's Tea Stall for a cup of tea, on the way back from the classes where we discussed all kinds of stuff. Unfortunately, Ramdhani is no more now- may the noble soul rest in peace. Now his sons are keeping the tea legacy alive. The first semester went off very smoothly like a breeze.

Then came the second semester in October 1983 after a short break. On the studies front, we never lowered our guard and kept pace with the class routine excelling in class tests but it's a fact that all the main festivals fall during the second semester period. It was always alluring to add a couple of days here and there to the closed holidays and make quick trips to your hometown. Incidentally, I even tied the knot in November 1983 in the middle of an ongoing semester like a true multitasker! Naturally, I had to avail myself of a few days' leave. I had missed the regular classes but I was keeping a close track of my attendance so that it doesn't fall short.

As luck would have it, I caught fever on a trip to my hometown and this made the difference- towards the end of the session, I came to know that my attendance in this semester had fallen short! Incidentally, our professors also couldn't complete the course in three subjects since the curriculum was quite heavy, so extra classes were being held to cover up the unfinished courses. Despite this, I missed the qualifying attendance by a whisker- just a couple of days.

It was distressing for the two of us who had a short attendance and we were called upon by the Director of the School. While we were in his chamber, he offered us seats but demanded an explanation. He had seen our applications requesting a waiver which were accompanied by our respective medical certificates. One by one, we explained to him how our attendance fell short, mainly the last moment illness. As we spilled our tales of woe, he eyed our medical certificates sceptically, muttering, "*Earlier it was Rs. 2, now it's Rs. 5, you can get such certificates from anywhere.*" Classic bureaucratic humour!

At this my senior colleague who was with me retorted proclaiming our status as sincere students who had done remarkably well in the first semester and in all the class tests of this semester as well. He continued that we were responsible government executives and not ordinary students, that we would try such tricks. I threw in the cherry on top, reminding the Director that our selection for the course was a testament to our impeccable integrity. After a while, the Director looked convinced, perhaps accepted the arguments, and allowed us finally to write the examinations!

Just to share, I passed my examinations in *First Class with Distinctions* and surpassed my first semester performance. ISM, Dhanbad, has since donned the prestigious IIT crown, and I, my friends, proudly wear the badge of an ISMite. It's one of the premier educational institutions of India. Our alma mater has a very strong alumni association that shares an enduring bond amongst the old pupils.

So, here's to the peculiar tales of academia, medical certificates, and the enduring camaraderie of being an ISMite. *Really proud to be an ISMite!*

Sudanese Sojourn

After an exhilarating round of golf on a Saturday morning in January 2003, I made a brief stop at the shopping center within our Baroda office-cum-residential complex. It was there that I ran into an IT colleague, who informed me about a fax message received the previous night from the Delhi office. The message was for me relating to an interview scheduled in Delhi the following Wednesday for an overseas deputation.

I knew that ONGC Videsh (OVL), the overseas arm of ONGC, had acquired oil and gas blocks in Sudan from the Canadian company 'Talisman.' The forward plan involved ONGC and OVL executives replacing the Canadians in the oil fields and offices over the next 2-3 months. Sudan, plagued by years of civil unrest, made the prospect of a posting there daunting. However, orders were orders and to be followed. I touched down in New Delhi on Tuesday evening and checked into a hotel booked for me by my office.

In the morning, I arrived sharp at 9 am for the interview at the pre-designated venue. Vinay from HR was orchestrating the entire process. He informed me that I was the first candidate on the list for interview. Vinay, who later became a friend, often chuckles when reminiscing about our brief conversation that day. He recounts that, despite conducting numerous interviews, he had never encountered someone who said, "I can't afford to perform poorly in the interview but please make sure I don't get selected. Guess who it was? None other than yours truly.

The Selection Committee comprised the Managing Director, OVL and Director (Exploration), ONGC. My interview lasted for almost 30 minutes and I came out satisfied with my performance. Much to my surprise, within less than a month, I found myself receiving marching orders to relocate to Khartoum! I wasn't keen to move at that point in time since my kids were at a critical academic juncture where they would require me by their side, hence requested the Director to re-consider my posting during one of his subsequent visits to Baroda. He patiently listened but advised me not to miss this *once-in-a-lifetime* opportunity. In a lighter vein, he quipped that Lady Fortune seldom knocks on the door and if ignored, she moves on leaving her daughter behind—Miss Fortune (misfortune)! While I wasn't thrilled at the time, I later realized the sincerity in his advice, acknowledging that this international posting significantly altered my perspective on work and life.

Word spread like wildfire in ONGC work centers about officers being deputed to Sudan, the newly acquired Asset. Most were relieved they didn't have to go, primarily due to newspaper reports detailing frequent civil unrest in the region. Colleagues approached me with sympathetic looks, offering words of encouragement, assuring me that I would emerge unscathed from the posting! Despite the concerns, I packed my bags and embarked on my journey to Khartoum via Mumbai and Dubai. At Mumbai airport, I met two more colleagues from different work centres, bound for Khartoum like me.

We were welcomed at Khartoum airport by our protocol officer who happened to be an ex-defence officer of Sudanese army. The Khartoum airport was very basic in those days and security checks were stringent. The yellow fever vaccination certificate was checked and despite the luggage having been passed through the X-ray machine, it was opened and checked thoroughly and passengers frisked, it took more than an hour by the time my turn came. My assignment placed me in Khartoum, working within the GNPOC Consortium (Greater Nile Petroleum Operating Company) comprising four national oil companies: ONGC from India, CNPC from China, PETRONAS from Malaysia, and SUDAPET from Sudan. As the Team

Leader for two oil exploration blocks, I led a multi-national team of geoscientists from these companies.

The learning curve began on day one in the office. Needing a couple of technical reports, I approached GNPOC's Operations In-charge, an exceptional Malaysian production engineer. Introducing myself, I requested the reports, and he welcomed me with a warm handshake. Seated, he jestingly remarked, "Yes, Mr. Sharma, why not. You will surely get these reports." When I inquired about the collection time, he smiled and said, "I am the custodian and now that you require them, you become my client. I am duty-bound to provide them to you as soon as possible. By the time you walk down to your desk, they will be in your mail's inbox." True to his word, upon reaching my desk, the inbox gleamed with two messages containing the awaited reports. Such dedication and efficiency left me amazed. The level of sincerity, commitment, and dedication witnessed that day was a profound lesson for me. In the early 2000s, the company embraced a *'paperless office concept,'* conducting all work online. The lone ball pen I brought from India returned with me after 15 months with less than one-fourth of its ink used—a testament to the efficiency of the paperless approach.

We took residence in the same apartment building that once housed our Canadian predecessors.

For a brief period, there was an overlap where some Canadians continued their roles in the office and field, facilitating a smooth transition. The building comprised over forty well-maintained studio apartments, managed by an efficient housekeeping staff under the caring supervision of an elderly Russian lady. All our studio apartments were well appointed with ample facilities. The campus had a swimming pool with heating facility, a well-equipped gymnasium, a TT table, a tennis court, Pool table, a piano, a golf practice net, etc. An elegant restaurant with an a-la-carta menu was operated in the building by the local staff. We also had a country office in Khartoum with a Country Manager- a senior executive from ONGC.

We were surprised to know that Khartoum had over a thousand strong Indian diaspora then, mostly from Gujarat. The Indian community settled in Sudan (now about 1500) dated back to the nineteenth century. As in most other geographies, the Indians enjoyed a good reputation in Sudan also. A local Sudanese from my team told me that his septuagenarian grandmother would watch Bollywood movies all through the day on her VCR every day. Indians are popular there as a non-interfering and peace-loving community since the Indians never took sides in their long history of ethnic conflicts and civil war.

Khartoum, which means *'Elephant's Trunk'* is the capital of Sudan, located just south of the confluence of Blue and White Nile rivers. Both rivers are huge and it's a treat to watch the confluence. Interestingly, India's Chief Election Commissioner Sukumar Sen oversaw the first Sudanese parliamentary elections in 1953. India provided financial support to the Sudanization Committee established in February 1954, which was tasked with replacing British staff in the Sudanese government, post-independence.

Confluence of Blue Nile and White Nile- the difference in colour of water is remarkable

Our Sudanese colleagues used to say that when Sudanese law fails, the Indian law is referred to!

Within three months at GNPOC, all the Canadians had departed, and we had seamlessly assumed control of the positions they had vacated. True to our Indian nature, we readily extended assistance and guidance to the Sudanese nationals. We went beyond the norm, visiting offices even on holidays to delve deeper into local geological technicalities and ensure our local colleagues understood the intricacies of the issues at hand. The Indians quickly gained popularity among the nationals. In contrast to our predecessors, we not only resolved issues but also took the time to explain the details and finer points to them.

As part of our routine, after returning from the office each working day, we would spend an hour chatting with our families back home, locking ourselves in our respective apartments. My stay in Khartoum brought numerous learnings. A special thanks to Director (Exploration) Mr. YB Sinha, who is no longer with us today—may his soul rest in eternal peace. I will always be grateful for his invaluable advice not to miss the colossal opportunity of a lifetime, in Khartoum.

Even a short stay of just fifteen months significantly broadened my perspective. Working alongside people from diverse nationalities, all converging in a foreign land for a common unified objective, proved to be a rewarding experience. Interacting with them, sharing experiences, and attempting to learn a new language—Arabic—made for an exciting adventure.

Though I came back to India in fifteen months time once my tenure was over, our company thrived, achieving an acquisition cost break-even in just two years, surpassing the estimated four-year period! Another feather in the Indian and ONGC cap.

Blissful Bogota

Embarking on my second international assignment after a brief stint earlier in Khartoum, Sudan, I found myself in the enchanting city of Bogota in Colombia. Assuming the role of Country Manager and Legal Representative for the Company, this posting was both sought-after as well as demanding. The challenge lay in the fact that, despite a few wells being drilled in the past eight years, none of the company's five exploration blocks in Colombia had yielded any commercial oil or gas discovery.

My predecessor in Bogota was a highly skilled professional and an adept administrator, bringing extensive experience in oil and gas operations. He managed the company's affairs effortlessly. Upon my arrival in Bogota, spanning a journey of nearly 13,000 kilometers with a layover in Frankfurt, I was warmly received by a colleague at the airport and was escorted to a hotel. On May 15, 2014, I commenced my duties in the office, overlapping with Dr. Sharma, my predecessor for 14 days before his return to India upon reaching superannuation.

During this period, I familiarized myself with various aspects of the role. Following Dr. Sharma's

Arrived in Bogota!

departure, I diligently completed all the local statutory compliances necessary for a new *'CEO and Legal Representative'* to assume the role legally in this Latin American nation. Over the next fifteen days, my wife joined me, and we transitioned into a comfortable apartment.

By this time, I had taken into grasp quite a few things. Nestled at a staggering altitude of 2625 m above sea level, Bogota sprawls across 1600 square kilometers, boasting a vibrant population exceeding 8 million. It proudly holds the title of being the world's largest city at such lofty heights. This mountainous town is a captivating blend of history, culture and natural beauty. What makes

Bogota truly remarkable is its climatic marvel. Wake up to a brilliant, sun-kissed sky in the early morning, witness a gentle drizzle in the late forenoon and then a refreshing breeze under a blue sky interspersed with scattered white clouds. The temperature delightfully between 12 to 24 degrees centigrade all through the year makes this a very pleasant place to live. Being a Spanish colony for long, the official language here is, unsurprisingly, Spanish.

The famous Bolivar Square

Bogota city, known for its rich cultural heritage defied the shadows of Colombia's past conflicts. The conflict of recent times witnessed since 1964 had settled and with the peace agreement between the revolutionary forces and the government ushering in a new era of peace and development.

Bogota had emerged as a vibrant hub, celebrated for its stunning architecture, street art scene, pulsating nightlife and is also the financial and commercial centre of Colombia. It is home to many museums namely, Gold Museum and National Museum that showcase Colombia's rich history and culture. Some of its famous landmarks included Monserrate Sanctuary, Bolívar Square, La Candelaria and the nearby Zipaquira- the salt cathedral.

Zipaquira- the Salt Cathedral

Another interesting landmark is Guatavita, a sacred lake of the Muisca, indigenous people predating Spanish arrival. Zipa, the ruler of 'Bacata' (now Bogota), offered gold to gods, floating adorned in gold on Guatavita. The rituals and gold found at the lake's bottom likely inspired El Dorado tales.

Gutavita Lake of El Dorado tales fame near Bogota

Colombians are known for their love of life and positive attitude. We found that they have a remarkable ability to be happy and positive, even in challenging circumstances. The only barrier that we initially thought would be the communication since neither my wife nor I spoke or understood Spanish- the local lingo. I did not feel the squeeze because I worked and moved in an English-speaking environment. The real challenge was for my wife but surprisingly she picked up Spanish very fast through a few local friends. It was great fun listening to their conversation- her friends speaking in Spanish and she communicating with them in English! It was more of expressions and hand gestures that helped her communicate till she picked up Spanish and later became comfortable with it.

Our car chauffeur Senor Nelson, a gentleman par excellence, had a great role in making our lives simpler- a friend, philosopher, and guide in the true sense of the term. He knew everything that one would like to ask about in a new place and was consistently there to guide us.

Lake Neuasa- famous for boating and camping

In my exploits, I've discovered that sometimes being a bit clueless about the local language can actually work in your favour. Here's an interesting tale. Like in many countries, in Colombia also one must undergo a medical checkup for enabling the social security cover under the Country's health care scheme. One fine morning, I found myself at the designated health clinic at the crack of eight. The staff nurse on duty walked me through the entire procedure and handed me a schedule that seemed to stretch through long hours.

They started with blood works on an empty stomach and offered an orange flavoured drink to prepare me for the postprandial blood test after 2 hours. I waited for a while then I was gracefully ushered into the ECG room.

Once over with the ECG recording, I took the ECG strip from the technician's hand and started examining it from one end to the other, like the doctors do. I had learnt basic reading of an ECG from a tutorial long ago and just wanted to see if I could identify any abnormalities! The technician was observing me with a mix of surprise and curiosity. She asked me questioningly- *doutor from India?* (Doctor from India? in Spanish). I didn't respond to her but I was slightly nodding my head as I was looking at my ECG record on this narrow slip of paper. She probably thought that I was nodding to her query and picked up the intercom and spoke to someone with great enthusiasm, I noticed. From that point onwards, I didn't have to wait for any of the remaining tests. I was received with visible enthusiasm in all the departments and was subjected to tests on priority. Lastly, when I reached the General Physician for consultation on all the tests carried out, he welcomed me and asked about my specialization.

He knew English very well. I told him that I was a geologist by education and a petroleum explorationist by profession. He said, "Please repeat", which I did. He chuckled and said, "For a moment I thought you said that you were a gynecologist! Our staff was quite amused since morning when they confused you for an Indian doctor when they saw you reading your ECG and this was there on my the back of mind also." So that was it- an interesting incident!

In another month's time I was able to find my feet and was comfortable in this new overseas

A replica of Taj Mahal in Colombia

assignment. Leading a stellar team comprising five Indian executives and five Colombian executives working with me, I decided to join the *Agencia*

Nacional de Hidrocarburos (ANH). This strategic move helped me get acquainted with the CEOs of other oil and gas companies operating there. Their insights into local petroleum geology and the ebb & flow of oil/gas trends proved to be invaluable. I stayed in Bogota for almost fifteen months, thereafter, summoned back to New Delhi.

The great teamwork at the Bogota and New Delhi offices including ONGC's Institutes in Dehradun, Ahmedabad and Baroda finally broke the jinx and a commercial oil discovery of significant size was made in Colombia. The experience lingers in my memory and has become a cornerstone of my professional journey. Bogota was a short but remarkable stay. We still cherish the days spent there and the great successes that we had there, subsequently.

Ultimately, its true that teamwork harnesses the collective power of a group, transforming individual contributions into a synergy that propels the entire team toward success- our success in Colombia is a testimony to this.

Epilogue

Congratulations! If you have reached this last page of the book without skipping much, I must say that you have lots of patience and you are a great reader. As I conclude this journey through a series of real-life stories, we're reminded that life's most cherished moments often lie in the unexpected and the unscripted. The anecdotes I have shared are but a glimpse into the boundless human experiences. The reference and context to almost all the anecdotes covered under this collection somehow hover around my career related circumstances.

As we part ways, may you carry with you the laughter, tears, and wisdom found in these pages. Let these anecdotes be a source of inspiration and a reminder that the world is full of wonders waiting to be discovered in the most ordinary of places. I must appreciate your appetite for knowledge and deep love for literature, making you an inspiring and admirable reader. Your passion for books is truly commendable.

Cheers!

Sudhir

www.ingramcontent.com/pod-product-compliance
Lightning Source LLC
Chambersburg PA
CBHW021402150726
47989CB00005B/2362